D1273938

Schumann

ANDRÉ BOUCOURECHLIEV
Translated by Arthur Boyars

Schumann

Evergreen Profile Book 2

GROVE PRESS
NEW YORK

JOHN CALDER
LONDON

Schumann
by André Boucourechliev

Contents

Introduction

What strikes one most after a careful reading of Schumann's writings – his intimate journals, autobiographical sketches, correspondence, literary and critical essays – is their enormous wealth of contradictions.

This apparent incoherence has been used by some as the evidence of his early derangement. Others have built their theory out of the very diversity of the material Schumann has bequeathed to us: every preconceived idea about his personality can bring into focus a number of features which remained constant throughout his entire life. For every idea of Schumann, sane or insane, careful or chaotic, mystical or ironic, has helped to create a different portrait of the man, and the results, usually concoctions, are seldom accurate.

But one of the advantages of modern literature is that it has exploded the theory of the 'coherent personality'. Even before Joyce or Pirandello, man had been shown as an alchemy of contradictory elements: it was surely because of his grandeurs and miseries, his misdeeds and his follies, his weaknesses and his heroics that he appeared even worthier of the interest which we call 'love'.

And so, who was Schumann? He himself helped us to find out by possessing such an acute awareness of his own multiplicity. He can be found in Eusebius, Florestan and Master Raro, their mediator. Schumann was all of them. His music helps us to understand him even more than his writings, for this was his real work, and in it we can find essential evidence of the division which lay between the light and dark sides of his nature. Schumann's inborn multiplicity was already revealed in his earliest compositions such as the *Papillons* (Op. 2). A game of masks, in which every moment had its anguished core, *Papillons* was also a game of mirrors in which man desperately sought to find himself, concealed behind his countless faces.

It was in the great fresco of German romanticism that this many-sided genius rediscovered a strange unity. Schumann, the most romantic composer of them all, collected and ennobled the tormented desires of his elders. Their art, different but one and the same in its pursuit, had nourished his genius. Schumann was truly the fruit of this poetic tree, and it would be wrong to deny the connection. He was without doubt the last of these whose destinies sought no delay once they were accomplished. He was one of these hallucinated spirits, ripe for an early death because of their rejection of an imperfect world in which the clocks could not be turned back. He was, in fact, one of that unhappy race who, in their search for the infinite, ventured not only their work, but even their lives and their reason.

Zwickau in 1813

A provincial bookshop

Romanticism was a revolution – a total revolution. It overthrew at one and the same time the sensitivities and ethics of an epoch, its art forms, its literary, philosophical and religious thought. For those who dedicated themselves to it, it was like a conversion. No country adhered more absolutely to its tenets or brought as much genius to its shrine as Germany. And one might say that everything that was of consequence in that country, from 1770 right up to the end of the nineteenth century, was romantic. Embracing everything and with powers of endurance, German romanticism, although it tended to be more 'carried away' in some of its aspects than either the English or French varieties, was still capable of more light and shade than is generally believed. It knew how to convert a certain classicism to its own purposes, and assimilate it without losing its own impetus.

It would be ambitious, even ridiculous, to attempt in a few pages to give an account of German romanticism. Nevertheless it is impossible to avoid this task when one is about to embark on a study of Schumann. For Schumann not only brought romantic music to its zenith, and was through his personality, his inspiration and his destiny a romantic figure *par excellence*, but he also responded as a fervent initiate to all the appeals of his epoch. He dreamed of becoming a writer in the following of Jean-Paul Richter. As a journalist, he took up an aggressive attitude in

11

(Karl Spitzweg)

The house where Schumann was born

favour of the romantic composers, lashing out at the 'Philistines'. His sensibility and his art had been shaped by the poets and the thinkers whose works formed the *credo* of Young Germany. For this reason we must present these fellowfighters, these innovators, these spiritual brothers of Schumann.

When Schumann, who was born on the 8th of June, 1810, in the small town of Zwickau in Saxony, discovered the life of the spirit, the romantic movement in literature had already produced its finest masterpieces. These were the books which Schumann discovered in his childhood on the shelves of his father's bookshop, and which his father talked to him about when he made him partake in his work. The father whose melancholy and bizarre temperament made him prefer working in his study to looking after his shop, devoted himself to a literary career. In spite of the obstacles provided by his provincial bookshop, he was a tireless writer of gloomy tales about knights, and translated and introduced Byron and Sir Walter Scott into Germany. He also belonged to the 'Sturm und Drang' movement.

12

(Moritz von Schwind)

Goethe

Schiller

In the second half of the eighteenth century, 'Sturm und Drang', the romantic *avant-garde*, set itself up against the negation of everything that had drama and mystery, the rigid discipline, the scepticism of heart and spirit of which the 'age of enlightenment' had witnessed the triumph. Now the most important need was no longer to *see* but to *believe;* to believe in genius, in innocence, in the sanctity of love or nature; to believe in man's mission, in the irresistible power of his inspired action. Schiller had been the purest originator of this renaissance. He had restored his greatness to the hero and his passionate sincerity to the romantic. So as to live one had to go through flame, and as this epoch could not accept the gift that was too great for it, the middle ages were revived and an imaginary world was evoked where terms like love and death, battle and freedom were given their weightiest meanings. All was demanded, all was allowed, all was possible.

Into this heroic flank of the 'Sturm und Drang' movement Goethe (to mention only one aspect of his prodigious genius) managed to introduce the rehabilitation of sensibility in connection with the simplest everyday things. But sensibility did not mean affectation in this context, and these idylls often had tragic conclusions which made their characters into heroes. The mild sentimentality of the 'Vicar of Wakefield' was renounced once Werther had committed suicide.

14

Jean-Paul Richter

A contemporary of Goethe and Schiller who, although not as great, had a more profound and prolonged influence upon the young romantic generation than either of these two giants, was Jean-Paul Riehter. Ever modest, and for long completely unknown, this prolific writer, only occasionally brilliant and often altogether confused, had a style which seemed in places to be jumbled up in the most absurd manner. But in his work, in a nebulous form, was to be found all the most contradictory of romantic themes hopelessly entangled. He wrote an idyll about some poor, simple country folk, in which the spirit of compassion was as tear-provoking as the irony was acute. Through their innocence and love of nature these humble people had a revelation of mysteries of the most elating or the most terrifying nature. At one moment, the whole earth seemed to accompany their amorous ecstasy with a fantastic exultation; at the next, in an icy cemetery, the resurrected Christ announced to the souls that all hope was lost and that nothing existed apart from this desolation. The most seemingly delirious of his stories are charged with symbols uncompromising in their purity. Because of this power of transfiguring the universe considered as a mystic harmony, and the reconciliation of irony and tenderness, of the prosaic and the profound, Jean-Paul had become the precursor of the strangest and the most extreme aspects of romanticism. All the young

15

'*Two men watching the moon*' (*C. D. Friedrich*)

poets knew him and venerated him, and the young Schumann made him his idol.

Jean-Paul's successors clarified these trends and involved themselves body and soul in their quest of the absolute. They were in every sense the heroes of the romantic movement, and of all the themes which they illustrated so fantastically, there was not one which they had not actually lived.

Their torment expressed itself in an absolute repudiation of the present and a feeling of nostalgia for an everlasting never-never land. Even while they sang of the beauties that were most accessible, such as the harmony of a landscape, or the innocence of a child, they made it seem like a mysterious world revealed to the poet alone, and of which all the 'Philistines' ever saw was the common appearance.

> . . . . . They feel thee not
> In the golden flood of the clustering grapes,
> In the dark juice of the poppy.
> They know not it is thee
> That enfoldest the delicate maiden
> And makest her heart a tender paradise!
>
> Novalis ('Hymns to the Night')

16

(*Moritz von Schwind*)

Travel was one of the most frequent themes of the period. After Goethe, Uhland, Chamisso and Eichendorff journeyed on foot along the roads of the old Germany, still rich in its evocations of the middle-ages. Journeys in space and time, idle or melancholy rovings, these trips satisfied the thirst for solitude at the very heart of nature, or the temptation of the unforeseen that lay, perhaps, beyond the next twist of the path.

From these travels which brought the poet into contact with the people's soul unsullied by the age of enlightenment, Arnim

and Brentano brought back the 'Wonderful Horn', a collection of simple poems and ballads whose tone was either sweet or harsh. Following them, Eichendorff and Uhland found there the inspiration and the unstudied form of their own poems:

> Those whom he loves as his own sons
> God sends through the vast world
> Wishing to show them all its wonders...

But the greatest of them undertook entirely different journeys, fantastic and adventurous ones of the spirit which led to the very doors of death or madness. Novalis was the first to explore the gloomy kingdom of night and examine the most hidden mazes of the earth where, at the heart of the metals, lay the secret law of the universe.

'He is the master of the earth, he who sounds its abysses ... in his eyes, in the night of the gulfs, gleams an eternal ray...'

He invoked the night, and the night heard him. Aged twenty-nine, and in love with the idea of an early death, he vanished.

Kleist, after having brought romantic drama to its feverish climax, mingling dream and reality, consciousness and prophecy, also yielded to this destiny of death, and at the age of 34 committed suicide, taking with him at the same tragic time the girl he loved. Hölderlin, the greatest of the romantic poets, was engulfed by madness and for thirty-six years, surrounded by silence, was the attentive prey of a poetry which could not be translated.

What imitators were created by these extreme destinies! How many forgotten names could one add to those who made their hopeless wager on the irrational to achieve the conquest of the most profound mysteries. And how many of these heroic

Novalis
Hölderlin
Hoffmann

starts were engulfed in madness or in death, or, worse still, in mediocrity.

This frenzied quest for another land, ever more deeply penetrated, took on a novel form in the cases of Hoffmann, Tieck and Chamisso. They also explored, beyond the boundaries of the obvious, the secrets of the universe, of the spirit and the heart. But the anguish of their search was often quelled by irony; the might of their fore-knowledge was marked by the whimsical humour of a story with a magical signific-ance or action. Schumann who, like them, worshipped at the shrine of Jean-Paul, was impregnated by their passionate and pro-found vision while still a child. He found in Goethe's 'Faust' and in Chamisso's 'Peter Schlemihl' the obsession of man's irreconcilable duality; in Brentano and Arnim a world full of angels and devils and in Hoffmann the fascinating and tragic personality of the musician Kreisler.

To these insatiable beings who were not afraid of being burned by any revelation, reason itself seemed feeble, and intuition and prophecy in their turn showed them-selves to be inadequate. Words were im-perfect utensils, and even poetry remained too bound up in the bonds of language. All these poets aspired to an art nearer the soul, and nearer the supernatural. Their inspiration was of an entirely musical nature. They invoked the spirit of music, and their heroes were often possessed by it.

Lessing, the philosopher, Hoffmann and Tieck, in particular, declared that a fusion of the arts in which music was 'the wonder-ful interpreter of the inexpressible' would be the most perfect state. With the su-preme revolt against rationalism, music opened out as a domain without limits.

'When carried away by emotion, I

Ludwig Tieck
Clemens Brentano
L. A. von Arnim

wish to express it, it's not words I look for, but sounds.' (Jean-Paul Richter)

A young disciple of Jean-Paul who believed himself to be a poet, wrote at the age of seventeen: 'It's strange that just when feeling speaks most strongly in me, I have to cease being a poet.' The writer was Schumann.

The universe which Schumann discovered as a child from his voracious reading did not appear to have marked him in any way. He was radiant, carefree and calm. His mother called him 'Lichter Punkt': 'point of light'. Robert worked with Kuntsch, the organist, a mediocre though honest musician, and seemed to be generously gifted for music, and at the same time hardly less so for literature. His curiosity and his imagination were always on the alert. Sociable and open-natured, he shared his early enthusiasm with everyone. But in these happy gifts no one dreamed of discerning the mark of genius or the sign of a mighty vocation.

He owed the musical shock of his childhood to one of the most marvellous of the pianists in the period which abounded in virtuosi. He was nine years old when his father took him to Carlsbad to hear Moscheles. On their return, Robert, overwhelmed with enthusiasm, demanded a piano. Henceforth this was to be his chosen companion, the confidant to whom he could open his heart, and the interpreter of his changing moods.

As a child he did musical caricatures at the piano. As a young man he gave himself up to improvisation which sometimes finished in the shedding of tears. Later still, it was to the piano he took to confiding his most intimate, personal and poignant inspirations.

It seems that his father had noticed that the boy possessed more than mere facility. He dreamed of entrusting him to Weber, but that great musician had left Germany for England. If his idea had been realised, would Schumann have been able to start developing his marvellous genius while still a child? Perhaps he would have been spared a great number of vicissitudes and uncertainties. But he had to find himself, with difficulty and with pain.

At the age of twelve, Robert formed a small orchestra of his playmates, composed a psalm and studied Mozart, Haydn and Weber. But it was literature that still attracted him most strongly. Byron gave him a feeling of exaltation. Goethe, Schiller, and Jean-Paul Richter in particular elated him. He knew 'Faust' by heart, and so well that his school-friends, whom his enthusiasm spared no recitation, nicknamed him 'Faust' or 'Mephisto'. He also founded a literary society where the boys of his age would learnedly discuss the classic and romantic authors. He had already written short essays, a dissertation on art, and poetry in the style of Jean-Paul such as the 'Miscellaneous Writings of Robert de la Mulde' and, later on, 'June Evenings and July Days'. However, nothing as yet permitted his genius to be foreseen or demanded that an exclusive choice be made.

Right up to his fifteenth year, Schumann, without abdicating the charms and the privileges of childhood – spontaneity and variety of enthusiasms – developed for himself, and, without any restraint, a sensibility and a taste that were astonishingly diverse and romantic. It was only when his period of adolescence was over that there appeared the dilemma of his double vocation.

Suddenly he became withdrawn, indifferent and melancholy. Another world seemed to open up in him, an unknown torment became master of his being. He had had a presentiment of it without understanding it: now it lay revealed as the devil which haunted the early romantics – nostalgia, foreboding, and the desire for a universe beyond one's reach.

'Earliest youth experienced these moments when the heart could not find what it desired, for, darkened by an inexpressible nostalgia, and by tears, it knew not what it sought. It was

21

something silent and sacred in which the soul could feel its rapture, when the youth made dreamy question of the stars... ('June Evenings and July Days,' Zwickau 1827).

For Schumann, as for every other romantic, to penetrate this universe, *to go still further*, meant to create. Work was the confession of an original torment, but the creative act was the attempt to gain ascendancy over it. Now that the young man had woken up to this summons, his desire to create became all-demanding. Art, for the first time, appeared to him as a grave obligation. Situated between two uncertain vocations – poetry or music – he was struck by the need for a choice. However, the days passed in indecision. The dilemma which confronted him, instead of tending towards a solution, only became a more unhappy one during these years.

The first portrait ...

22

Schumann's father

'...What I really am, I do not know myself ...If I am a poet
– for no-one can become one – destiny will decide one day.'
(Intimate Journal, Zwickau).

It was then, in 1826, that Schumann's father died. In him
Robert lost his surest friend and a faithful and understanding
guide, who could alone sustain him in his slow-ripening vocation.
The youth's inner confusion found an unhappy reproach in his
grief and he abandoned himself to morbid fantasies, to melancholy and to a strangely passive state. His improvisations at
the piano, once full of spirit and animation now brought tears
to his eyes.

In his reading of Jean-Paul, Schumann sought not an appease-
ment, but an obliging echo to his torments. Jean-Paul had the
most profound and total influence over him. He was the master
of his thought, his literary model and the constant example
in his life. 'In many respects', wrote Marcel Brion, 'Schumann
was a character out of Jean-Paul. The reason he admired the
heroes of his novels so greatly was because he found that they
were his soulmates and that he recognised himself among them...'
Jean-Paul and Schumann dreamed of the same ideal world and of
the same mystic brotherhood between men. But what struck

Schumann to his very core was the constant presence of music in his master's work. Even more than in the case of the other romantics, music played the greatest role in this work. Its task was to translate the most ineffable and mysterious sentiments before which poetry was impotent. In love with the inexpressible, Schumann nevertheless believed himself destined to pursue a literary career. He started two novels and three plays, influenced by the author of 'Hesperus', which remained unfinished. In Gustav, the hero of one of his attempts at novel-writing, he sketched this portrait which might have been his own: 'Gustav loved what was above the earthly, what was mysterious spirit. And so it was that he had the revelation of the 'Double' before he had ever heard anyone speak of it... His ideas on music and art: the plastic arts – painting and sculpture – were placed on a lower plain than the spoken arts like music, poetry and drama. In the universe all was movement. This was why an *adagio* or slow movement created a far greater feeling of tension... Don't rebel at the thought that there are so many tears in life: do you renounce the dissonances and the minor chords in music – don't you in fact love them? They both of them bring us heavenly delights...'

Like the heroes in Jean-Paul, Robert plunged himself in the contemplation of nature. He took long walks, which were full of ethereal outpourings in the manner of Jean-Paul, Nanni or Liddy, his first loves. He recited them long passages from '*Hesperus*' or '*Titan.*' And if Liddy did not seem inclined to worship at the shrine of the great man, with what a wrench of the heart was the mocking girl sacrificed, but with what superb conviction!

'... I had plucked a rose and was just about to give it to her when the thunder and lightning set the east aflame. I took the rose and stripped it of its petals. The burst of thunder had wakened me from this sweet dream. I had returned to earth. Liddy was seated facing me, her blue eyes filled with tears. Sadly she contemplated the savage menace of the clouds. I could still have said to her: "That's just what our life is like". But we left Rosenburg without uttering a word. When I took leave of her, she clasped my hand firmly; the dream was over, and the sublime image of the ideal vanished when I thought of the things she had said about Jean-Paul.'

Deeper still, and more productive than these childhood idylls, was the love Schumann offered to Agnes Carus. Cultured and

24

musical, she introduced Robert to a world full of poetic overtones. It was the world of Jean-Paul, but it was also the world of Schubert which she revealed to the young man. Schumann, whose adolescent enthusiasms were principally literary, discovered in Schubert the initiator of musical romanticism who was nearest to his own nature. 'I did not speak freely about Schubert,' he wrote much later, 'or rather, I only spoke of him to the trees and the stars...'

Despite their intimacy, Agnes Carus, older than Schumann and married to a Codlitz doctor who was a friend of his parents, remained

an inaccessible and sacred object of his love. But he had found in her the first incarnation of the 'eternal feminine', and at a moment when he had hardly sought his path she had turned him towards music, which was to be his destiny. 'Her divine image shines in my soul, eternally holy, and in my heart, in her presence, there awaken new melodies', he wrote; and, years later, in a letter to Clara: 'I loved her once, passionately ... she represented my ideal among women.'

Robert Schumann was eighteen. Even if he had written nothing besides the titles of novels and a few musical sketches which he soon abandoned, he found himself at the end of his brilliant studies full of ardour and confidence in the future.

In March, 1828, he wrote to his friend Flechsig: 'Now the world lies before me. I could hardly restrain my tears when I came out of school for the last time. But, in spite of everything, my joy was far greater than my sorrow. Now having reached man's estate, I must show what I am. Thrown into existence, in the night of the world, without guide, master or father, nonetheless the universe has never appeared to me in so rosy a light as at this moment when I face it, free and joyful, and defy its storms...'

This freedom which elated Schumann was nevertheless only that which came from indecision, and its result was of short duration. Did not his turbulent soul seek rather a chance to be committed? Undecided regarding his creative vocation, he

25

accepted with a docility that seems astonishing an entirely alien solution, and one which was chosen for him. Schumann was to become a lawyer; the decision had been taken by his mother. And so he left for Leipzig not as a wandering poet, or as a musician, but as a student of law.

Without setting too strict limits to human greatness, nevertheless I should not rush to count Schumann's among the more ordinary natures.

He had talent for many things and none for others. His temperament: melancholy. His artistic sense: a greater aptitude for feeling than for observing. Also in his judgments, in his creation, he was subjective rather than objective. Emotion came more naturally to him than effort. So as to understand things he preferred to abandon himself to his instinct rather than to his reflection. His intelligence was more abstract than practical. His imagination was powerful, turned inward, but often seeking its inspiration from outside.

This man who possessed sagacity, artistic sense, a strong memory and not too much irony, who felt more than he reasoned, was dedicated to art, not to speculation. Excellent at poetry and music, he was not, nevertheless, a musical genius. Both arts were equally dear to him. Jean-Paul had influenced him greatly.

As a man he was distinguished for his taste, his tact, his lack of timidity, the forcefulness of his spirit, his lovable nature and his artistic gifts. He pleased whom he wished. Though he was firm when the argument was heated, he seemed remote in mediocre company. He liked to mock such people, but he also knew how to attach them to him. He was not brimming over with genius. Struggle was unknown to him, also he preferred to dream in silence.

His love was pure and sacred. He had loved many with a noble and divine passion. He knew that young girls found him pleasing. For him the world was not a garden of delights but a temple sacred to nature. He was religious but had no religion. He loved people and was not afraid of destiny. I should like to depict his soul, but alas I do not know it in its entirety as he has enveloped it in an impenetrable veil which only the years could dissolve.

Such was Schumann at this time.

The 'Juridicum' of the
University of Leipzig

I must show what I am . . .

In the year 1828 Leipzig was one of the most important cities in Germany, and one that was proud of its university and its intellectual and artistic life. Instead of finding it full of the affection of his fellows, and its atmosphere charged with sympathy and admiration as it had been at Zwickau, Schumann found it too distant from nature, which had been his friend and consolation in his darkest days. It was there that he served the apprenticeship of solitude and experienced the impotence of his indecision. It was there also that he acquired the lucidity and courage demanded by a choice that grew more necessary from day to day.

Robert fell in with his mother's wish for him to go in for a profitable career, but he found out very soon that the study of law bored him. He followed the courses and worked in fits and starts but only, as he admitted, *mechanically*. His spirit was never fired by the arid study of jurisprudence, and even though he brought an interest, fostered by his good faith, to the philosophy course, his true bent still lay in another direction. Besides Schumann was too refined, too self-demanding, to devote himself to the student-life of the period, made up as it was, of drinking-bouts and duels whose ritual behaviour was fastidiously regulated by the local authorities. To tell the truth, these disciplined shows of violence disgusted him. He held himself apart and retired into a world of his own, composed of friendships, dreamy reflections

29

Schumann's mother

St. Thomas's Church at Leipzig

and music. More than ever before music became his confidant, his refuge, his heart's need, and a revenge for the spirit freed at last from extraneous bonds. Without revolting against his circumstances and his obligations as a student, Schumann saw to it that the best part of himself was given to music. In this respect he was indebted to the historic city of Leipzig for a rich beginning. At Zwickau Robert had only known a *milieu* consisting of provincial amateurs, and the training he had received had been undisciplined and incomplete. Whilst at Leipzig, in addition to the concerts at the Gewandhaus and St. Thomas's Church where the tradition of J. S. Bach was perpetuated, he could frequent the musical societies and the homes of enlightened music-lovers. He met Dr. Carus again, now Professor in the Faculty of Medicine, and the beautiful Agnes, and found gathered around them the most eminent musicians of the day. Once in touch with them, Robert began to ask himself questions about his own capabilities: he wished to take stock of himself as a pianist and composer. Left to himself he wanted to get clear of the facility and superficial *brio* which had characterised his adolescence, and he chose the hardest means for excelling at what was still merely his pleasure.

Acting on the advice of Agnes, he sent his earliest compositions to Wiedebein, a conductor on the look-out for youthful talent, and an admirer of Jean-Paul. In Jean-Paul's best manner Schu-

30

mann introduced himself as one of music's neophytes, an impulsive pupil of nature, impatient to burst all his bonds, while modestly admitting that he knew no harmony and understood nothing of counterpoint. 'Work, young man', was Wiedebein's reply, 'and cultivate your generous gifts.' And so our youthful lawyer placed the 'Well-Tempered Clavier' by Bach on his piano, and made his daily bread out of this rigorous study.

It was also at the Carus' that the young man met Wieck, whom he had to reckon with over the years, and who changed from the venerated teacher into the persecutor of his favourite disciple, and the tormenter of a budding love. This despotic teacher of genius revealed to Schumann the requirements of pianistic technique, and the need to provide a solid basis for his fiery inspiration.

Wieck, whose birth had been humble, loved music. Without a great vocation, but ambitious, he had by sheer tenacity and self-denial, acquired his musical education and experience without the help of others. Having discovered that his talent lay in teaching,

he became the best known piano teacher in Leipzig. Who could yield better to his pedagogic fury than his own daughter? Since her fifth birthday, Clara, a born musician and an obedient child, had been the guinea-pig in his experiments, and the example and the living advertisement for his method.

When Schumann heard the child, then aged nine, play at the Carus', the demonstration must have been a convincing one. The impressionable musician decided to place himself in Wieck's charge knowing that in him he could find no indulgence or tolerance for his romantic outpourings And so after the friendly chamber music sessions, where enthusiasm was respected more than pedantic exactitude. Schumann learned to put up with a severe apprenticeship lasting many months.

This asceticism which was purely musical, since his legal studies were willy-nilly and his life generally in disorder, was swept away by a sudden feeling of instability, an abrupt need for freedom and change. He wanted to leave Leipzig, to get away from the noisy atmosphere of Saxon students and leave Wieck whose lessons already appeared too astringent for him.

This was not a rebellion. Schumann remained a docile, if not an industrious student, and it was by pleading his interest in his studies that he asked his mother to install him at Heidelberg. He was attracted by the enthusiastic letters from his friend Rosen who studied law there. Two great authorities, Thibaud and Mittermayer, were professors at the university; life was calmer, and the intellectual and artistic tastes more refined in this ancient and aristocratic city than in Leipzig. In addition to the charms of the town and its cultured atmosphere, there was the fact that it was right next to nature. And so Robert departed. His was a true escapade, 'a flight across a multitude of spring skies'. And on his journey Schumann appeared to us in his perfect guise as a young romantic traveller, greedy for sights and sensations to which he could respond from the very depths of his being.

For him, Frankfurt was 'thousands of young girls strolling down avenues flowery with spring gardens, and the lovely River Main bearing barks and small boats on the mirror-like nape of its neck.' It was also a memory of Goethe and the evocation of Ariadne at Naxos. As he could not resolve to leave a pleasant fellow-passenger he accompanied him all the way to Coblenz where for the first time he saw the Rhine, 'the holy river', which he followed right down to Mainz.

'The fine ruin of Ehrenfels looked down proudly on me and on

32

the Mauseturm. The sun set majestically, and then all was suffused by the calm of twilight. On the Rudesheim shore lay boats at anchor, astir with life and movement. Beautiful children were playing gaily on the river's edge and with such animation that I almost missed the moonrise. An old boatman and daughter took me into their boat. Not a ripple stirred the water and the moonlit sky was an incredibly pure blue. Rudesheim with its dark Roman ruins were reflected in the waters, magically transfigured by the moon. My heart overflowed ... I called to some alongside. The silver moon shone constantly, and the flowing tide of the Rhine softly closed the eyelids of the weary traveller.'

Travelling by post-chaise, Schumann received the confidences of a secretary of the Prussian Embassy, and the effusions of a dancing-master dressed in grey. He heard the tale of the Battle of Waterloo told by an old Dutch adjutant. He was asked if the weather wasn't wonderful? He then installed himself in the coach-man's seat and drove the carriage feeling 'in a divinely joyful mood.' Was there a storm threat during their departure from Mannheim? He left on foot, prophesying a wonderful sunset and

'The children in the forest' (Karl Spitzweg)

at nine o'clock he arrived at 'his longed-for Heidelberg', carrying his bundle on his shoulder.

He only stayed there a short time, in fact only long enough to learn Italian, and in the summer of 1829 he set out for Italy. His friend Rosen, who was to have accompanied him, bowed out of the trip and Robert left alone, and on foot. His purse was almost empty, but he was happy: 'This journey on foot has been magnificent and not tiring, thanks to the beauty and the continual diversity of the scenery. I tramped along in solitude, my knapsack on my back, swinging my alpenstock in the Alpine wind and stopping every moment to look behind me and engrave on my spirit the image of this wonderful paradise...'

He crossed Switzerland, skirted around Lake Maggiore and stopped at Milan where he heard Pasta, who aroused his ardent admiration. At Venice the little money he had left was stolen, and from that point onward his home-sickness began to grow. 'I am a distant and isolated traveller who has only his heart with which to speak, laugh or weep...'

Schumann, who was too young and very German, did not experience the revelation from this 'round-trip', that Goethe had before him. His impressions were highly-coloured but superficial, and Italy, for him, was a memory, not an inspiration. But it was a poetic and musical memory which revealed him to himself as growing constantly more of a poet and more of a musician.

At Heidelberg the authority and originality of Thibaud's thought had made him take renewed interest in law. But, although he declared in certain letters to his mother, sometimes with determination and sometimes with melancholy regret, that he no longer thought about the piano, his sojourn was brightened by music. He would spend long hours playing for himself, alone in his room, or with friends. He played at the house of Thibaud, his Professor – an illustrious and unhappy example of a thwarted musical vocation. He was even heard in Mannheim by the Grand Duchess Stephanie of Baden, invited there because of his reputation as a pianist.

'You will find it difficult to imagine', he wrote to his brother Julius, 'to what extent I am loved at Heidelberg and also, I can say without flattering myself, to what extent I am thought of and esteemed. I have been baptised 'The Public's Favourite'. My popularity dated, of course, from a concert at which I played the 'Alexander Variations' by Moscheles. The applause and the calls for a repetition would not stop.'

In a letter to Friedrich Wieck, to whom he owed the revelation of his talent for the piano, he was even more open:

'If only you knew the ardour, the ferment that is in me and how I should have already arrived at Op. 100 with my symphonies, if only I had written them down! There are moments when music possesses me so completely, when only sounds exist for me to such a degree that I am unable to write anything down.'

As possessed as he was by music, Schumann remained the prisoner of a paradoxical situation: he was faced by a middle-class future

which disgusted him and a destiny which seemed to have been imposed on him. But he did not know how to choose the one he should veer towards. When would he put an end to this contradiction, this doublelife of which one part was a useless sacrifice to obvious social necessities, and the other, an inadequate commitment to art and genius which could be satisfied only by the gift of the whole?

What was needed in the year 1830 was an event, in the nature of a shock, to bring this about. But Paganini's concert, which he heard at Easter in Frankfurt, and which doubtless renewed the vivid impression he had gained when, as a child, he had heard Moscheles, only received the briefest of mentions in his journal which was usually so verbose. Schumann refused the bait of incitements which might have bought him to a speedy decision. The revelation of his true calling resulted only from a series of whims, chances and uncertainties. His literary facility and his many attempts in this field had not impelled him to become a writer; his sense of filial obedience had not turned him into a lawyer, and his meeting with Wiedebein and his apprenticeship to Wieck – not to mention Paganini's mighty impact – did not commit him to consecrate himself, without reservation or withdrawal, to music.

However, after every desertion, music appeared more clearly to him as his natural mode of expression. And when, finally, by bursting all his inner and outer bonds, Schumann made it his choice, it was hardly a choice but a slow and inevitable approximation of his genius. After so many wanderings between the calls of instinct and the false demands of reason, and after so much hesitation about the literary or musical nature of his creative aspirations, Robert Schumann, free from all immediate pressures, at last formulated his destiny for himself. His letter of July 30th, 1830, so often quoted, shows us a new man, clear-minded and resolved. To his mother, whose decisions had so long weighed him down, he wrote kindly but firmly of his irrevocable intention.

'My life has been for twenty years a struggle between poetry and prose, or, if you prefer, between music and law... At Leipzig, I dreamed and loafed, I lived without discipline, and, to tell the truth, I was unable to bring off anything that was of value. Here I have worked better, but here, as in Leipzig, I feel myself irremediably dedicated to art.

'Now I stand at the cross-roads and the question "Where shall I go?" frightens me. If I can follow my genius, it will guide me towards art and, I believe, on to the right road. But – do not feel hurt if I say it quietly and tenderly – it has always seemed to me that you barred my way.'

Christina Schumann was overwhelmed by the way her youngest son had escaped the destiny which she had dreamed of for him, and which she had attempted to impose on him with a kind but implacable obstinacy. She felt close to death and for a long time, she admitted much later, she was unable to pray. The whole of Zwickau was in a state of ferment over this matter, and only the aged Kuntsch sent the rebel a token of confidence and esteem, the encouragement of his grandiose predictions.

Robert demanded that Wieck be the arbitrator and accepted his verdict in advance. The eminent pedagogue's appreciation did honour to his judgment and at last brought back Christina's approval. Wieck promised her that in three years he would make her son into a pianist 'more spiritual and more fiery than Moscheles and more magnificent than Hummel.' The family storms died down, calmed by Robert's tact and tenderness and the disinterest he had shown while in his brothers' company regarding his share of his late father's estate. Schumann lingered at Heidelberg – a pleasant relaxation after this internal crisis and the ensuing struggle – and settled the debts he had accumulated as a student. In October 1830 he set out for the grim town of Leipzig, the new objective of his dearest desires and the reward for a hard-won victory.

'I am devoting myself to art,' he wrote to Wieck on the 21st of August, 'I want to devote myself to it, I can, and I must do so. I am taking leave without a tear of a science which I could never love. It is not without qualms that I look down the long road which leads to the goal I have set myself. But, believe me, I am determined, and I have many reasons to be. I feel that I have courage, patience and the necessary faith, and I am ready to work. I trust you implicitly and place myself entirely in your hands...'

He moved into Wieck's house, and enthusiastically began on the six month's trial period demanded by his mother in her obstinate anxiety. But it was a hard road to follow. In his correspondence and his intimate journals ardour alternated with discouragement, and the elation of work with attacks of hypochondria. At times he dreamed of surpassing Moscheles and becoming the Paganini of the keyboard. He would shut himself up for whole days in front of his piano, and would be bent over the most thankless exercises and the most tyrannical demands made by Wieck. At other times he was indifferent to everything, a misanthrope, and felt 'his heart empty and dead like the future.'

'There are days', he wrote in his journal, 'when I see oppressive clouds passing over every face – or is it my inner gaze which makes me believe I see them?... Don't let yourself be depressed, dear Robert, when the scales on your piano are not as rapid and as pearly as they were the day before. Work patiently, lift your fingers smoothly, keep your hand calm and play slowly: everything will come right...

'Yesterday it went very badly at the piano, as if somebody were holding back my arm, I didn't want to force it. Trouble and darkness seem to submerge beings and clouds alike....'

On days like this, a desire to create, which had not yet been properly realised within him, would revive his courage, He dreamed of composing, of writing a romantic opera on 'Hamlet', in which setting it would be 'all fire and flames'. He overflowed all day with 'sweet and fabulous melodies. The thought of glory and immortality gave strength to his imagination.' In spite of his dark moods and his discouragements, now, more than ever, the music in him did not stay silent.

But these spontaneous outpourings were no longer enough to satisfy his creative urge. He lacked the rudiments of the necessary musical training to express himself fully, and so in July 1831, he asked for composition lessons from Heinrich Dorn, director of the Leipzig Theatre, and a distinguished musician and theorist. Schumann quickly realised that this instruction revealed great gaps in his knowledge.

'I feel I am now acquiring that beautiful clarity which I had some inkling of before, but which was very often lacking in me,' he wrote to his mother. His musical intelligence became more refined, but he was quick to discover the limitations and even the dangers that lay in over-formalised conceptions, and in January 1832 the young romantic again rebelled. 'Dorn

Friedrich Wieck

and I', he confided to Wieck, 'will never agree. For him music is simply a matter of fugues.'

The rupture took place, provoked by Dorn, but the lesson had not been lost. 'I admit', he wrote in the same letter, 'that these theoretical studies have done me good. Before, everything seemed to be born out of the inspiration of the moment. Now I can follow the play of my enthusiastic thought, stopping now and then in the middle to mark my position.'

And so Schumann pursued an independent course. If he collected, and even solicited, the advice of his elders, he did not linger long with any of them. It was among the great dead masters that he sought his guides. He made a particular study of the works of Beethoven and Schubert, for whom his admiration had been purely instinctive up to that time. He went constantly deeper in his researches into Bach, 'that genius who purifies and gives strength', and who remained his true master for the whole of his life.

As earlier on, the authority of Wieck weighed heavy on Schumann. Always a prey to the same instability, he already dreamed of leaving the master into whose hands he had placed himself entirely, so that he could go to work at Weimar with Hummel. But Wieck, who had painfully suffered Dorn's lessons, put him back onto the right road quickly and not without brutality. He had no intention of letting so talented a pupil add to the glory of a rival celebrity.

Schumann worked relentlessly. The piano was not obedient enough, technique was tiresome, and slow to come. Obsessed by the great example of Paganini and impatient to press on, he evolved the absurd notion of assuring the independence of his fourth finger by working with his middle finger kept immobile by a string.

In the spring of 1832 his hand was paralysed. Driven to distraction, Robert kept this accident hidden from his family, and took his hopes from one doctor to another, even having recourse to quacks. His house was transformed into a chemist's shop. Would he have to give up music? Right up to March 1834, he tried all the treatments with a fierce and desperate obstinacy, and hoped for a miracle. But his finger remained paralysed[1], and Schumann would never be a virtuoso.

This accident, which the biographers call providential, since it removed Schumann from the destructive fascination of a virtuoso's career and obliged him to devote himself entirely to his loftiest

---

[1] The third finger and not the fourth, as is generally stated. The fingering in the *Toccata* is explicit in this respect. It is thanks to M. Alfred Cortot that we can give this precise information.

'The dance of death', detail (Alfred Rethel)

and most personal vocation, made him suffer cruelly for a long time. Writing to his mother in 1834, he pretended to resign himself to the abandonment of his career: 'Don't give yourself any worry on account of my finger... I should hardly have been happy as a touring virtuoso; I would have valued a profession like that at nothing.' But years later he suffered desperately from this disability and from this obstacle placed in the way of his musical expression by a jealous destiny.

'Lord, why did you do just that to me?', he wrote to Clara in December 1838. 'In me the whole of music is so complete and alive that I should like to exhale it, and that I can only do painfully, with one of my fingers straddling the other. It is terrible, and I have suffered agonies from it up to now.'

This disability and these disappointed hopes were doubtless far from unconnected with the deep depression into which the young musician fell in the autumn of 1833. He was the prey of fevers and irrational fears, and passed from over-excitement into a state of prostration. When cholera broke out in Germany, Schumann immediately demanded his passport wishing to flee to France or Italy, and was so beside himself that his mother begged him 'Try to conquer your fear of cholera, for the fear itself might be a danger.' The deaths, which had been close together, of his brother Julius and his sister-in-law Rosalie – both of whom he had loved most tenderly – brought his neurosis to such a peak that on the night of October 17th he felt that he was going mad. With a presentiment

of the tragic plot which, twenty years later, was to finish with his exit from the world of mortals, he tried to escape madness in death, and by throwing himself out of the window.

After that he could not bear high staircases or the sight of sharp instruments – methods of suicide of which the unformulated temptation frightened him.

'Would you believe', he wrote to his mother in November, 'that I had not the courage to travel to Zwickau alone for fear that something might happen to me? Violent congestions, inexpressible fears, failure of breath, occasional fainting-spells, these all overtake me in quick succession, but less often, to tell the truth, than they used to. If you only had an idea of this sleep of the soul, completely exhausted by melancholy, you would surely forgive me for not having written to you.'

It was in 'a state of frightened debility', to use Robert Pitrou's strong expression, with all his bodily strength undermined, that Schumann dug himself in at Zwickau for the entire winter.

These years of crisis were not however completely overclouded and unproductive. Schumann had started his career as a musician, and his true genius as a creator was revealed through his doubts and his struggles. He now approached the supreme test, that of 'pain well-loved', which was the elaboration of a perfect and durable form.

His first works, conceived during his last weeks of contemplation at Heidelberg, and worked at during the time of his apprenticeship with Wieck, saw the light of day. The 'Abegg Variations' (Op. 1) were published in September 1831.

'If you knew', Schumann wrote to his mother, 'what these first joys of a composer were like. It would be right to compare them to the feelings of a bridegroom. All the sky of my heart is full of hope and joyful prophecies. The Doge of Venice, when he wedded the sea, was no prouder than I am when I celebrate for the first time my union with the vast world which is the world and the motherland of the artist.'

The 'Abegg Variations' translated the ardour of a young composer into an exploitation of all the resources of his instrument and his chosen form. They were brilliant and skilful, and despite some overtones of Weber, their character of spontaneity and imagination already bore the unmistakable mark of Schumann.

The dedication had a small deceit due to youthful vanity. The work was destined to convince Zwickau of the talent of the prodigal child; to this glory Robert, who was then frequenting the *salons* of the Grand-Duchess Stephanie, wished to add that of the young man already 'launched'. And so he dedicated the variations to an imaginary Countess Pauline von Abegg whose name was the theme (A – A natural, B – B flat, E – E natural, G – G natural).

A   B   E   G   G

It was to let it be thought that there were aristocratic intrigues and flattering favours which would properly dazzle the middle-class inhabitants of Zwickau. It is not known if they were dazzled, but even if the criticism was rather cold, Christina Schumann was impressed. And although she admitted that she could not follow his thought at all, she gave her maternal blessing to a genius whom at last she had recognised.

In contrast to the virtuosity of the 'Studies after Paganini's Caprices' (Op. 3), a brilliant homage of the 'Devil's violinist', was the delicacy of the changing nuances which besprinkled the 'Intermezzi' (Op. 4) dedicated to his friend von der Luhe. To his brother Julius, whose death shortly afterwards affected him so strongly, Robert sent his 'Toccata' (Op. 7) so that he might 'loosen his fingers.'

But the masterpiece of these early creative years was the 'Papillons' (Op. 2), a richer piece with a profounder significance and mystery than those I have just mentioned. His contemporaries wanted to see in it the joyful beating of light wings, when it was in fact the musical picture of an internal world where Schumann already revealed himself in the opposition of his 'doubles'. The work followed the episodes of the fantastic masked ball which ends the 'Flegeljahre' by Jean-Paul. A copy of the novel, annotated in Schumann's hand, a letter, and these words: 'The clamour of the carnival dies away, the clock in the tower strikes six' written on the last lines of the score, all go to show that in one of his earliest works, the young composer had tried to bring about through feeling that union of music and poetry which had haunted all the romantics, and Jean-Paul in particular. To this evocation Schumann brought the tragic obsession which was his own: a game of doubles, a game of masks, a terrifying sense of the artificial excitement and the vain agitation of a fête – as many symbols of the impossible meeting as people.

45

Davidsbündler against Philistines

Schumann slowly emerged from the state of prostration into which he had been forced by the terrible crisis of 1833, and, having overcome his confusion and his feeling of having been diminished by the paralysis of his hand, he returned to Leipzig. He plunged afresh into the exciting life of the German musical capital, and the former solitary now fled solitude and sought the lively contact of enthusiastic artists. Every evening Robert was at his table at the 'Kaffeebaum', his beer in front of him, his cigar in his mouth and enveloped in a cloud of smoke. His passionate warmth and his irony attracted people to him; his occasional silence and melancholy, as well as the mark of genius which he bore, made them remain. Wieck was there, occupying the seat of honour with all his authority as an eminent teacher, and all the vigour and the rather brutal severity of his thought. Knorr, an old Bohemian pianist, full of passion and imagination, Lyser, the painter, author of the 'Northern Thousand and One Nights', but also a musician and a man of the theatre, Schunke, handsome but consumptive, would all join with him in endless discussions. The 'regulars' of the 'Kaffeebaum' surrounded them, musicians, poets and journalists whose names are now forgotten, but all in love with music, provided it was bold and authentic. These were all Schumann's soul-mates. They all burned with the same convictions and with the same ambitions.

It was Schumann who proposed the idea of a modern musical

47

review to the group at the same moment as the 'Gazette Musicale', to which Berlioz and Liszt were contributors, was kindling a revolution of taste in Paris. The musicians took over criticism, and genius claimed the sole right to pass judgment on genius. In Germany at that time an old officer, a magistrate and a pastor, mean and envious people and ignorant imposters where beauty was concerned, were the musical critics who decided whether a work deserved success or notoriety. Their bad taste as well as their bad faith were infallible and they managed to stifle every voice which did not agree with their dismal ideals. Schumann, who in 1831 had started an article on Chopin in the 'Allgemeine Musikalische Zeitung' with these words: 'Hats off, gentlemen, here is a genius!', was not asked to contribute again to this highly serious paper. In the musical world the 'Philistines' occupied all the strong positions. They controlled not only the newspapers, but the publishing-houses and the conductors' desks. On all the operatic stages, Rossini and the Italians, 'these canaries' Schumann called them, ruled like potentates. On the piano – though who they were eludes us – one heard only Herz and Hünten. Chopin and Mendelssohn were just starting to be successful, but exerted no influence as yet. Thalberg and Hummel were the only really considerable names to be included in concert programmes. Bach and Beethoven had been banned from them, and Schubert and Weber, hardly gone, were also forgotten.

What the people with youth and talent needed was a war-machine and above all it was necessary to deprive of their malevolent monopoly the sneering censors who inundated genius with their sarcasms. And it was Schumann, a young and unknown composer, who founded the 'Neue Zeitschrift für Musik' (New Musical Review) and led the attack of the *Davidsbündler* in a new musical 'Sturm und Drang.'

Davidsbündler: What ties and mysteries joined the living and the dead together in a sacred brotherhood – the very real frequenters of the 'Kaffeebaum' with characters who were totally imaginary? Who were Eusebius, Florestan, Raro, Serpentinius and Juvenalis? Who were Jeanquirit and Saint-Diamond, Estrella and Zilia? At that time and in that country riddled through with secret societies, confederations and conspiracies, who were the adepts, and what was the purpose of the Association of the Companions of David 'which ran like a scarlet thread through the journal combining truth and poetry in a humorous manner?'

Schumann admitted much later, in the preface to his collected writings, that 'this Association was more than secret, having only existed in the brain of its founder.'

'So as to bring out different points of view on the questions of art, it did not seem a bad idea to me to invent opposing artistic characters, of which Florestan and Eusebius were the most important with Master Raro as the mediator between them.' But the *Davidsbündler* were more than a mystification destined to *épater le bourgeois*, or the fantasy of a youthful critic. Even if they had never existed save in Schumann's spirit, this would alone have sufficed to endow them with a burning reality. For at one and the same time they were the personifications of different shades and momentary contradictions in the musician's temperament as well as the spiritual family in whose bosom he flourished beside his equals. Bach, Mozart and Beethoven belonged to it, as well as the Frenchman Berlioz and the Pole Chopin, 'without any certificate having been awarded to them'. The friends of the 'Kaffeebaum', founders of, and contributors to, the 'Zeitschrift', had their place in it: Wieck, under the name of Raro, (which Schumann also gave to the arbiter between the differing extremes of his personality), Schunke, Lyser, Heller (the mysterious Jeanquirit, the Paris correspondent of the review), Mendelssohn (Mentis), and Richard Wagner, a composer as yet unknown, who sent in the most astringent reports. The brotherhood had its muses: Livia was

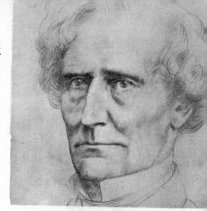

Berlioz (drawing by Legros)
Chopin (drawing by Winterhalter)
Wagner (after Tichatscheck)

Henrietta Voigt

Ernestine von Fricken

Henrietta Voigt, Schumann's 'soul in A minor', for whom, as earlier for Agnes Carus, he felt a tenderness akin to love, and Ernestine von Fricken, whom he was engaged to for a short time, became Estrella. The names of Chiarina or Zilia concealed one and the same young lady: Clara Wieck, the little pianistic phenomenon whom Schumann had heard demonstrate the excellence of her father's method, and whose entry in his *Carnaval* he marked with the direction 'appassionato con molto anima'.

50

Clara Wieck (Fechner, Paris, 1832)

To the band of *Davidsbündler* charged with 'fighting to the death against the philistines of music, and the others', Wieck-Raro issued this proclamation in the review in the manner of a General about to go into battle: 'Young people, the road you have to follow is long and difficult. There is a strange glimmer in the sky. I do not know if it is the dawn or the setting sun. Establish the light!'

Out of this glimmer Schumann created a dawn, the one which heralded the undisputed reign of musical romanticism. Here are some of the attacks, so full of spirit and conviction, (not to mention talent), with which our youthful champion confounded the mediocrities and stripped the cheats of their false glory:

Neue
Zeitschrift für Musik.

Herausgegeben

durch einen

Verein von Künstlern und Kunstfreunden.

'Works are needed for every level of culture. The only things which must be excluded from art are hypocrisy and ugliness, which disguises itself with seductive veils. It is these polygraphs to whom creation is only a question of money (and there are distinguished names among them), these vagrants, these poor and poverty-stricken simulators who clothe their need in tawdry finery, whom we must fight with all our strength.'

On a 'Fantasia' by Heinrich Cramer, he wrote: 'There is nothing to wonder at in the fantasia, save that it has been remembered and written down by the composer... If the time should ever come – which publishers will curse if it does – when copying machines, adjusted to the instrument, will secretly transcribe the piece that has been played, such fantasias will appear in millions...'

On the occasion of Czerny's three hundred and second work: 'However diligent the critic may be, it is quite impossible for him to catch up with Herr Czerny. If I had enemies and wanted to destroy them, I would condemn them to listen to nothing but music like this...'

On Thalberg: 'The works of Thalberg have always received severe judgment in this review because we thought we discerned in him a talent for composition which his vanity as a virtuoso was dooming to destruction. But today he has quite disarmed us. His piece is not even worth the trouble of judging by our usual criterion.'

On a certain Herr Ruckgaber: 'Those who are in favour of a fusion of the German and Italian styles will find their dreams realised here. Take a bass with a triplet figure in tenths, sing a melody at the same time, and throw in a consumptive rubato, and the German-Italian school is ready...'

On Meyerbeer's 'Les Huguenots' which certain contemporary

critics considered as good as 'Fidelio', he wrote, in a long analysis which was an act of defiance against the prevalent taste: 'To startle or to tickle is Meyerbeer's favourite rule, and one he carries out successfully with the rabble. It is at one and the same time calculated and empty, superficial and "deep". Unfortunately it is impossible to deny that he has some wit, and we also know that he possesses an entire treasury of forms. One can recognise Rossini, Mozart, Hérold, Weber, Bellini, even Spohr – in short, the whole of music. Truly, let us thank heaven that nothing worse can come after this, unless we turn the stage into a gallows.'

But something worse did come, and here is Schumann's article about it:

'Le Prophète' by Meyerbeer
February 2nd, 1850
†

Meyerbeer, caricature by Dantan

Such was a dreamer's strength in battle. But this satire was not only made up of pungent epigrams. Even when it was brief, the analysis was as just as it was percussive, and the critic did not allow himself to be carried away by his verve; his reproach and contempt remained within bounds.

Schumann, however, also knew how to mix praise and reservations with a light touch. Writing of an 'Overture' by the English composer Sterndale Bennet, whose talent lacked breadth but not finesse, he said: 'Someone who does not already know this work should think of a bouquet. Spohr provided some of the flowers, Weber and Mendelssohn also contributed, but the greater part came from Bennet himself, and the way in which he arranged them is very much his own. It is not profundity or grandeur which touch us here, but finesse, that winged attribute which marks our heart with its light but lasting impression.'

Or on one of Hummel's later works, when, earlier on, the composer had been considered among the great, and now was no longer in the front rank: 'Even if time, which also casts its shadow on art, substituted for this clear mode of expression a form whose outlines were not so well-defined, tinged more with mysticism, let us wish not to forget the wonderful days when Mozart was king – and which Beethoven was the first to shake into violent motion.'

Having gone to war against the Philistines, Schumann often halted to give encouragement to some ideal companion in his struggle. Never were wit and taste less negative, for paradoxically enough, admiration gave joy to this polemicist who was only pitiless out of necessity. He himself admitted that when he found pleasure in a thing, he was all too ready to turn mere approval into praise.

It was in his enthusiasm that the chosen role of the critic lay revealed. Schumann has subtly analysed the difficulties of musical criticism when he was not content to offer merely a description of external features, or a simple reference to the theoretical rules, however relative. It was unable to prove what it asserted, and no criterion was imposed upon it by the nature of its object, since: 'Music is an orphan whose father and mother no-one can name', and 'men are overcome with a particular shyness when they are in the place where genius labours. They would be frightened if they were allowed to understand the genesis of a work.' What, then, were the methods, and what ought to have been the intentions of a critic worthy of the name? 'For us', Schumann replied, 'the best kind of criticism is the one which produces an impression comparable to that of the original.' No longer a dissection which only

seemed to explain, but a work of art in itself, criticism had to reflect and refract music. Like the music itself, it was aimed at the sensibility and the taste; its effect was produced by sympathy. And that is why the freest and most personal of forms was chosen by Schumann for the articles whose subjects were closest to his heart. This was not a beginner's lack of constraint, or uncontrolled effervescence, it was a deliberate choice of the most appropriate and convincing style. In literature and in painting, the romantics had shown themselves to be as penetrating and as innovatory as critics as they had been audacious as creators. In music, Hoffmann – who was also a composer – had prepared the way for a passionate, subjective criticism. It remained for Schumann to follow it through to its destination: his poetic vocation and the receptiveness of his sensibility, together with his wide culture and the subtlety of his musical judgment, all pointed to him as the founder of this *art*, which became criticism.

In the 'Neue Zeitschrift für Musik' the works admired were evoked in lasting or impassioned apostrophes, dazzling dialogues between Eusebius, Florestan and Raro, concentrated reveries broken up by a hint of irony, and a thousand-and-one comic rallies, rather than being submitted to crude dissections.

' "The Rage Over A Lost Penny", a rondo by Beethoven: What could be merrier than this jest? In spite of myself, I laughed from beginning to end while playing it over for the first time. It is the most harmless, aimiable rage such as one feels when one can't get one's shoe off; one perspires and stamps one's foot while the shoe looks up phlegmatically at its owner. Now I have you, Beethovenians, who swoon and turn up the whites of your eyes as you cry in exaltation: "Beethoven always sought the sublime, and freed from earthly cares, he flew from star to star!" His favourite expression when he felt in a good mood was: "Today I feel altogether unbuttoned". And then he would laugh like a lion and beat about him – untamable in that as in everything.'

On the subject of the erection of a monument to Beethoven: 'I go to No. 200 Schwarzspanierhaus and mount the steps slowly; nothing at all stirs. I enter his room; he rises like a crowned lion, but one that has a splinter in his paw. He speaks of his sufferings. At that very moment thousands of enraptured listeners wander beneath the temple pillars of his C minor symphony. Ah, if the walls could only spread out, he has a longing to escape, he complains that he is left alone and that people care little about him! At the same moment the basses stop on the deepest note in the *scherzo* of the symphony. Not a breath is heard. A thousand hearts are suspended by a single hair over a fathomless abyss; suddenly the veil is rent and the splendour of the highest created things builds rainbow upon rainbow. But we rush through the streets, and no-one knows him, or greets him... This is how you treated him in his lifetime. No disciple or companion offered to follow him.'

On returning from a concert, a performance of the '*Symphonie Fantastique*' by Berlioz, for example, Florestan perched himself on the piano, and expressed his enthusiasm in a few concise phrases; in language of unusual strength Master Raro reminded him to observe moderation, Jonathan interrupted him and Eusebius then launched into a strict analysis of the work, mainly intended to demonstrate how little light was shed by a critical examination, to point out some of the work's peaks to shallow souls, and, finally, to prove to those who grudged their admiration, that despite its disdain for the traditional, modern music was strong in construction and had a strong feeling for inner logic.

A form of criticism that was so novel quickly won over the public, and the young public in particular. The review soon had enough subscriptions for it to look fearlessly towards the future; all the time its influence was growing, and it became the rallyingpoint of many youthful talents. It was a heavy task for Schumann, who at first edited the magazine with Wieck's help, and then did it all by himself. Despite a brilliant panel of contributors, he was the author of a great number of the articles. For ten years he devoted an important part of his time to this crusade, to this musical conspiracy which he 'loved like a young fruit-tree which he himself had planted.'

'The Concert' (Moritz von Schwind)

Clara Wieck.

Two Lovers in The World

Dear and honoured Clara,

I know that you have a thoughtful nature and understand your mad old inventor of charades. And so I often think of you, not as a brother of his sister, or a lover of his mistress, but as a pilgrim of a statue erected on a distant shrine. During your absence I have walked through Arabia to find stories which might please you. There are six new ones about 'doubles' a hundred and one charades, eight very droll riddles, then there are some frightfully good adventure stories about robbers, and one about the white phantom which makes my flesh creep! My paper is coming to an end but not the friendship with which I am

Fräulein Clara Wieck's warmest admirer

R.S.

Clara was then thirteen years old and was a strange and rather unruly child with magnificent eyes. Robert was her greatest friend. He had lived for two years with the Wiecks, and once their hours of study were over, the little girl and the young man would seek each other out so as to play mad games or else go on long walks together. Schumann's journal is full of references to her: 'Clara showed herself to be mischievous ...At the zoo, Clara silly and timid... Clara more beautiful and grown-up ...Clara and I, arm-in-arm...'

This little girl was already a great artist. She went on brilliant tours during which 'each day was a blank' in Schumann's life, since he was deprived of his friend. She went from town to town and court to court inspiring admiration. Goethe declared that she had 'more strength than six boys put together', and paid her his homage by inscribing his portrait to her with a flattering dedication. A contemporary expressed wonder that 'beneath her fingers, the piano took on colour and life.' Although still a child, her genius as a pianist added something profound and slightly fairy-like to her make-up, and nothing escaped the fascination of this mysterious maturity mingled with the impulsive charm of the unsophisticated.

'To see Clara as she appears in the family circle, behaving ingenuously and childishly with her father and her relatives, one would think of her as a very pleasant young girl of thirteen, and nothing more. But if one looks more closely, one notices her fine and pretty little features, the slightly exotic eyes, the agreeable mouth which has an aura of sentiment and is sometimes contracted – especially when she answers you – in a jesting or woeful expression, also the graceful ease of her movements, not studied in any way, which would become someone of more than her age. All this, I confess, inspired me when I first saw her with a very odd feeling. It was as if this child knew how to tell a long story made up of pleasures and sufferings, and yet all she knows is music.'

This was how Lyser, one of the *Davidsbündler*, depicted her in the review 'Cecilia'. Even more than everyone else, Schumann fell under her spell. To the tenderness which the 'mad inventor of charades' felt for the little girl who believed with all her childish faith such stories as that he slept standing up, that he had a 'double,' that he always carried pistols on him as well as poison, Schumann added his genius' admiration for the child who, when confronted with the most majestic mysteries of art, simply 'lifted up her calm countenance towards them, when man might have been dazzled by their rays.' He looked on without envy as his young friend surpassed him in virtuosity, and, as a composer, he was the devoted admirer of this inspired interpreter: 'Clara played divinely ...I have never heard Clara play as she did today, everything she did was beautiful and masterly. She played the *Papillons* even better than yesterday... At home, played and worked at the composition of the *Intermezzo*. I want to dedicate it to Clara.'

The romantics had dreamed of these childish loves in which all forms of magic were mingled, where all was inexpressible and intangible, and remained unrealised. It was to Sophie von Kuhn,

62

a girl who died at the age of fifteen, that Novalis had dedicated his 'Hymns to the Night', the most beautiful poems on love and death to emerge from German romanticism. The stories, poems and pictures of the period are peopled with child-elves and child-magi whose divine naïvety was mixed with an intuition of the most poetic mysteries. Love was the only road which led back to the enchanted realm of childhood which all the romantics yearned after. Happy beyond all others, Schumann had lived in the company of an angelic child and musician while making this pilgrimage to the sources of life and poetry.

During these years of doubt and self-analysis, it was in Clara that Schumann found his joy in life, and it was from her that he drew the strength and peace necessary for his art. 'It is a pleasure', he wrote to his mother in 1833, 'to watch her gifts of heart and mind unfold ever more rapidly, and leaf by leaf. Recently when we were coming back from Connewitz I heard her say, as though she were talking to herself, "Oh how happy I am, how happy I am!" Who would not feel pleased to hear such words? Along the road there are some quite useless stones. As I have the habit of lifting my gaze during a conversation instead of watching my feet, she walks just behind me and gently pulls my coat before every stone so that I should not fall. Sometimes it is she who falls over a stone...'

After each separation their pleasant intimacy would start up again, and Robert's feelings grew more and more passionate. When Clara returned from Paris in 1835, she was sixteen years old. Robert visited her as soon as he could and suddenly realised he was in love. 'I still remember how I saw you for the first time at noon. You seemed more grown-up and stranger to me. You were no longer a child with whom I could have laughed or played, you said sensible things and I saw a deep and secret ray of love shining in your eyes.'

This love, once revealed, seemed to Schumann to have existed always. 'One person has dominated my life', he wrote a little later to Clara, 'and has drawn me into the innermost and deepest windings of her heart; it is her alone whom I have always venerated and cherished above everything... It was you who without wishing to, and quite unwittingly, turned me away from the company of women for years past.'

Eusebius was sincere, and certainly neither the little girls addicted to kissing with whom Florestan trifled, nor even Agnes Carus or Henrietta Voigt had penetrated to his inmost depths, as this child had done. Nevertheless at the moment of avowals, of the first kiss

64

and the first emotions shared, Eusebius, unless it was that scatter-brain Florestan, or the over-romantic Raro, Robert, in short, became engaged to another. The year before, while he was still suffering from the after-effects of the terrible crisis of 1833 and feeling greedy for affection, he had given his heart, which was secretly full of Clara, to Ernestine von Fricken, 'the finest girl in the world'. He had endowed this pleasant but ordinary young person with all the requisite qualities of a romantic beloved: her madonna-like purity, her goodness, her love for music maintained the rather artificial state of exaltation in which Schumann revelled. In this literary setting the young girl's sweetness and sincere love inclined him to see in her the beloved who also had powers of protection, and offered the feminine refuge which he had always needed. Everything conspired to bring about the conclusion of this idyll: Henrietta Voigt protected her, and Wieck, Ernestine's teacher and host, communicated with Baron von Fricken, enclosing an assessment of Schumann which was worthy of preservation: 'There is no limit to the number of things I could write about this rather fantastic person; headstrong he may be, but also noble, splendid, enthusiastic, wonderfully gifted, highly cultured and a writer and musician of genius.'

It was from this period that there dated the *Carnaval, scènes mignonnes sur quatre notes* (Op. 9), a masked fête: in the midst of fantastic or enigmatic personalities, the silhouettes of Florestan and Eusebius were inked in for the first time. For the first time Schumann expressed in the clearest musical terms the duality of his character, already certain, but unconscious, in the *Papillons*. From this time forward the melancholy *Adagio* of the one, and the *Passionato* of the other were the infallible hall-marks of Schumann's works.

Carnaval was the first work in which Schumann gave his genius full rein. Between the majestic '*Préambule*' and the final '*Marche des Davidsbündler*', eighteen episodes bore witness to a prodigal richness and variety of musical imagination. Four notes which were to be found at the basis of all these pieces provided the material for the most unexpected transformations. As in the *Abegg Variations*, they formed a name (A – A, E flat – S, C – C, B natural – H): Asch was the name of a very musical town situated on Ernestine's family estate. In '*Sphinxes*' these unplayable notes represented an enigma – dumb and mysterious, that joined Schumann's name to Asch:

In the episode subtitled '*Lettres Dansantes*' they took on life and body. Out of an imaginative vortex of buffooneries, pastiches and reveries streamed a parade of masks and portraits: Pierrot and Harlequin, Chopin and Paganini, Chiarina and Estrella beside Eusebius and Florestan. They crossed over, followed each other in a '*Promenade*', joined up again for a '*Valse Noble*'! The '*Aveu*' succeeded a '*Reconnaissance*'*:* the mystery of the sphinx, which remained unresolved, was a sentimental enigma. At last all the masks came together again for the *Finale*, in a warlike march full of the spirit of carnival. Then one recognised them as the *Davidsbündler* who, full of spirit and a cutting and impertinent ease, led a triumphant attack against the Philistines.

Ernestine's guardian, an amateur flautist, submitted a musical theme to Schumann; his simple and rather beautiful melodic line inspired the composer to exploit all the most orchestral resources of the keyboard and construct a work which fully deserved its name: *Études Symphoniques en forme de variations*. Starting with borrowings from others – the theme of the finale was taken from an opera by Marschner – Schumann created an original work of supreme unity; between the pretext for the work and the work itself, there was not a common measure.

These *Études Symphoniques*, (Op. 13), were indeed dedicated to transcendental virtuosity, but the purely mechanical difficulties were secondary, subordinated, as they were, to the more important problems of expressive interpretation; for a long time Schumann called these variations 'pathetic'. The character of the first *étude* is primarily rhythmical, accented by the contrasting of *legato* and *staccato* phrases; the second emphasised the eloquence of one part, by means of a simple accompaniment; the third recalled the tireless arpeggios of Paganini's violin. The perilous traps for the left hand in the sixth *étude*, the expressive polyphony of the eighth, the rapid passages in chords and the highpressure of the tenth made their appeal to the most varied resources of the instrument. But, in full charge of these experiments, Schumann saw to it that their results amounted to a beautiful and perfectly ordered work.

Carnaval, the product of a youthful amorous passion, was dedicated to the violinist Karl Lepinski, the *Études Symphoniques* on the theme by Baron von Fricken were dedicated to the English composer Sterndale Bennett. What, then, became of Ernestine? Although Schumann visited Asch several times, his possession by his exalted illusion never reached the stage of his officially demanding the young girl's hand in marriage. A letter to his mother lit up the unconscious reticence of this lover who was false in all good faith: 'If destiny were now to ask me which I would choose, I would answer without hesitating "This one." But that is faroff, and today I renounce the prospect of a closer tie, although I feel myself readily inclined in that direction.'

When, in April 1835, Schumann saw Clara once more, he became aware that Ernestine had merely paved the way for her arrival as the all-powerful sovereign of his soul. 'Ernestine's coming was necessary for our union', he wrote much later; and again: 'Ernestine is not unaware that she usurped your place in my heart, which loved you before it realised it.' Poor Ernestine, relegated to play the ungrateful role of the gardener in *Electra*, duped in the game of predestined hearts, and modestly helping to bring about the transitions! Robert was conscious of his faults but, incapable of simulation during these first months of a reciprocated love, found his tongue again, and Ernestine withdrew with a commendable good grace: the interlude was over.

During the course of the summer Robert's letters to Clara had changed from their tone of tender intimacy to that of a fast-ripening passion. The autumn was exquisite; daily meetings were resumed and were now charged with a more exalted quality and with a still deeper feeling of communion. 'Clara's eyes and her love...' Schumann noted in his journal; simply that, so greatly did her love for him, and his happiness, exceed what mere words could express. It was in the review, and sheltering behind the anonymous authorship of the 'Romantic Letters to Clara', that his exaltation saw the light of day.

The death of Christina Schumann, which happened unexpectedly in February 1836, precipitated the evolution of her son's feelings by increasing his solitude: 'Love me, love me well! I ask for much because I give much... Happily your radiant image dominates these shadows and helps me to endure everything.'

It was to Clara that the Sonata in F sharp minor (Op. 11), a work which had been started very much earlier, was dedicated

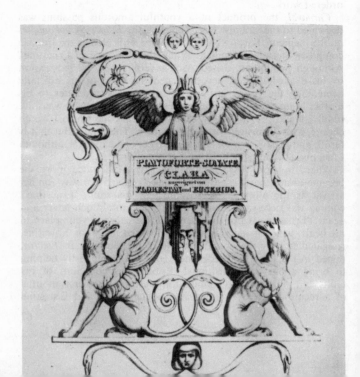

'by Eusebius and Florestan'. Schumann's inspiration poured forth with such abundance and such violence that the severe form of the sonata could impose no order on it. The work was more rhapsodic than architectural, and even more improvised than composed; but it was no less beautiful because of it. An '*Introduction*' in the form of a long, passionate and profoundly sonorous melody preceded the *Allegro Vivace* of a dance-like character. A tireless rhythm kept up its hollow beat in constantly contrasting *nuances* and suddenly burst into luminous showers of sound, proving its mastery over the entire register of the keyboard, and carrying off the invisible dancers on its whirlwind. Altogether different was the *Aria*, a song without words whose lyricism and poignant intensity did not yet come up to the disconsolate resonance found in some of Schumann's later works. A *Scherzo* full of contrasts, an *Intermezzo* '*alla burla*' led to the *Finale* whose dimensions, swollen by long repetitions, constituted an undeniable and triumphant proof of endurance for a sixteen year old pianist.

From this period also dated the Sonata in F minor (Op. 14), subtitled 'Concerto without Orchestra' by the publisher Haslinger, as well as a part of the Sonata in G minor, known as the second in spite of its later opus number. Between 1830 and 1838 Schumann did not cease working on it, so as to make it more perfect. He dedicated it to Henrietta Voigt. The G minor Sonata prescribed the dizzying rapidity of its *tempi* which accelerated still further inside each development in the instructions 'as fast as possible, faster, still faster'; very marked accents and the constant clash of brief and extended figures dominated the *Allegro* and the *Scherzo* of this fast-moving work. The *Andantino* seemed like a lull; this tender interlude, which owed the intensity of its expressive power to its very restraint, was one of Schumann's most beautiful passages.

In the *Finale*, movement was again supreme: the rapid striking of broken octaves created an impalpable and ghostly sound-effect. Little by little the colour assumed lustre, the intensity became more marked, and the speeding notes rushed headlong, irresistibly drawn towards a luminous conclusion. 'I am confident and I believe in our good genius. It is so long since I have known our

69

destiny.' This destiny which Schumann invoked with such certainty was suddenly going to be crossed by an inflexible will: Wieck intervened. The attentive father and the admiring friend, under whose eyes the idyll had been born, seemed suddenly to have sensed a danger. He reacted by making a prompt decision to remove Clara from the scene by sending her to Dresden. For the young lovers this was the first of those sorrowful separations which, for the next four years, would put their love to the test.

This opposition, which soon became fierce, found Robert incredulous and unprepared: 'He showed such a great preference for me, especially in the summer of 1835, when he must have seen our love ripening: he remained so long without showing hostility that I continued to be convinced of his benevolence.'

Simple Eusebius! He could not understand the whole of Wieck's possessive character. Like Hoffmann's hero who had constructed an automaton endowed with all the graces, Wieck, by his patient care, had constructed the precocious talent of his daughter. Clara was his masterpiece: in her he had awakened a musical genius; in her he lived the gift which had been refused to his awkward nature. And now a worthless musician was attempting to gain possession of this marvel by his passion; already the trap was opening of the love which would reduce the destiny of this prodigy to that of an ordinary woman. Married life and motherhood would destroy every trace of the gifts which had brought glory to this vestal of music, as well as to her creator. Wieck had brought his work to the pitch of perfection, but he had not exhausted the pleasures of pride and the satisfactions of the advantages which he had the right to expect. Rather than allow himself to be frustrated, he was prepared to persecute his daughter for sheltering a human attribute in her artistic make-up, especially if it were the most human of all. Angry, implacable and fierce, he was going to engage in a battle in which he would vent his rage in actions of the blackest wickedness and vilest ignominy.

All of a sudden, Wieck turned brutal. He forbade all interviews and messages. Clara was kept continually on tour, and when she returned to Leipzig her father kept a zealous watch over her. He had publicly broken off every connection with Schumann, he avoided the 'Kaffeebaum' and had given up the review. He set upon his old friend with slanders and insults. He employed himself in sowing doubt and discord between the young people: for Clara he painted the ruin of her career, obscurity, and misery, and suggested that when she was united with Schumann she

would be reduced to 'giving private lessons in clogs, under an umbrella.' He stirred up a rival of Schumann's in the person of Banck, the cellist, and was not slow also when it came to chasing him away! Schumann, he said, was fickle – had he not abandoned Ernestine? – and forgetful; the review wrote nothing more about Clara, and the humourous page on the pianist Ambrosia could easily have included a mention of her.

Schumann held firm in the face of this outburst. Sure of his heart and genius and convinced of their common destiny, he was ready for the most stubborn resistance; but dumbfounded at the same time, he did not stop hoping that an upsurge of the old affection would disarm Wieck's hostility. 'If only I had behaved badly towards your father, he would have the right to hate me, but I don't begin to understand why, without having a motive, he should detest and slander me, as you tell me he does. One day it will be my turn, and he will see how much I love him and love you.'

Without news from Clara, he did not know whether to doubt or hope, and his spirit was buffetted by the continual alternation of confidence and discouragement. As for Clara, exposed to the outbursts of a father whom she loved and respected, she sometimes had to give way. In June 1836 Wieck demanded that she should send Robert back his letters, and even the Sonata in F sharp minor which Eusebius and Florestan had dedicated to her. She obeyed in a moment of weakness and wrote the letter which her father dictated to her.

This was a terrible blow for Robert. He saw in this letter the proof of Clara's submission and, desperately, he tried to give her up.

'Being unable to learn anything about you, I wished, with all my might, to forget you. It was at that time that we had to become strangers to one another. I was resigned. Then my old suffering burst out afresh and made me wring my hands. Often at night I would implore God: "Grant me at least one night of tranquillity in which my mind would not give way." Once, I believed that I was going to find the announcement of your engagement in the newspapers, and felt as if my neck were being twisted towards the ground, and I cried aloud with the pain...'

At Leipzig, Robert felt abandoned; the *Davidsbündler*, unsettled by the dissension between their founders, were less intimate with him; Schunke, his dear friend, had died in the arms of Henrietta Voigt who also was soon to die of consumption. Schumann sought relief, or at least forgetfulness, in his work for the review which he now edited alone, and whose weight he sometimes found

The old Leipzig Theatre

overwhelming. He withdrew into his grief and 'could not speak to anyone, except towards evening, but mostly to his piano.' In improvising, which he had long since given up, he found the escape and at the same time the morose delectation which his obsession sought. He gave himself up to it as to a drug, and sometimes he even sought solace in drink.

From this period of despair and near-madness dated the great *Phantasie* (Op. 17), a work full of grief as well as hope and renunciation, and one of the most beautiful works ever written for the piano. Started in 1836, it had been Schumann's small contribution towards the monument which had been erected to Beethoven at Liszt's instigation. He announced it to his publisher as 'a Grand Sonata for piano entitled "Ruins, Trophies, Palms", of which copies will be sold in aid of the monument.' Then the sonata became 'three poems which I shall call "Ruins, Triumphal Arches, Starry Brightnesses".' However, it was not his pious desire to honour the genius from Bonn which inspired the work with its pathetic tone: 'it is nothing but a long cry of love for you,' Schumann wrote to Clara, 'you will not be able to understand the *Phantasie* if you cannot transport yourself in spirit to the unhappy summer when I renounced you. Now I have no more reason to

73

write such melancholy and unhappy works. The first movement is the most passionate I have ever composed, it is a profound lament on your account.' When the work appeared in 1839 under the title of *Phantasie*, only the dedication to Franz Liszt recalled Schumann's original intention.

The top of the score was inscribed with a mysterious quotation from Schlegel:

> 'Through the numberless sounds
> Which fill the world's gay dream,
> One song, barely heard,
> Calls to the secret listener.'

First Movement: – *To be interpreted in a fantastic and passionate manner.*

This 'long cry' which opened the *Phantasie* was one of the finest incantations in romantic music.

It unfolded and developed, then returned with a much softer sonority, as if a distant voice were echoing it. Again the call resounded, and this time a new theme answered it.

'This expressive theme is the one which pleases me most,' Robert wrote to Clara. Are you not yourself the song mentioned in the quotation? Yes, and you know it...' This second theme, in the minor, was led through a darkly-coloured transition to its transformation into the major and it was then that it revealed all its melodic richness. Two new transitional passages, with increasingly headlong rhythms, brought back the opening theme at the conclusion of this section, which appears to us like a single, immense musical phrase, so powerful are its impetus and its cohesion.

If Schumann was a romantic in the first part of the movement, he was even more of one in the second – *Im Legenden* with its nostalgia for another world – as in it he turned his gaze onto the fantastic wonders of the past. Here the poetry of sounds took on

an epic quality: soft and calm at first, it became more and more majestic as it took us deeper into this legendary world. One could make out the shadowy form of the 'theme of the quotation' (given above) caught in the rhythm of this new development. This rhythm asserted itself, became accentuated and abruptly broke its bonds, then hurled itself into a frantic race, now turned into a company of black knights. When this had disappeared into the distance, the opening theme was heard again, bringing with it the repetition of the first section. A short *Adagio* brought this movement of symphonic proportions to an end in an atmosphere of a fading dream and vision.

Second Movement: – The second panel of this immense triptych was a triumphal march whose implacable advance, tireless rhythmical persistance, and ever-increasing tension had almost an halucinatory effect. After the grandiose theme of the opening, whose heroic character was immediately asserted by the chords and, with the exception of a tender melody which brought a few moments' respite to the middle section, a single rhythmical figure:

underlay the structure of the entire piece, and impressed its obsessive persistence on it. The endless outbursts of such a figure were peculiar to Schumann, and were to be found times without number in his piano works such as the *Études Symphoniques* and *Kreisleriana*.

Towards the end of the episode, the high pressure of this hammered rhythm, blew up like a storm, as if time, the prisoner of a magic figure, had suddenly escaped so as to shatter itself against nothingness.

Third Movement: – A halo of sound, motionless and serene, was traversed by a ray of light, a descending melodic modulation which slowly displayed its changing rhythms. It passed and disappeared, melted into the grave harmonies of the opening and appeared once more. A new melody, less insubstantial and with greater warmth was imbued with restrained emotion:

it took on life, and then dominated the movement, alternating with the preceding themes. At last it burst out in a joyful rush and then vanished among intangible sounds.

The sombre melancholy of the first movement of the *Phantasie* found its answer in the *Davidsbündlertänze* (Op. 6) of 1837, a medley of contradictory sentiments, and reflected a divided soul and the period of torture when Schumann was being constantly cast from the exaltation of his love to the despair of separation and renunciation. More than the dances of the companions of David who, in former days, has assaulted the 'Philistines' in the *Finale* of *Carnaval*, these eighteen pieces were, Schumann told us, 'dances of the dead, dances of graces, and dances of familiar spirits.'

'At all times joy is mingled with sorrow', reads the proverb inscribed on the medal; but joy has rarely been so ecstatic, and sorrow so bitter. Aware of his self-laceration, Schumann signed every piece with an E or F, a useless admission, since the melancholy and the ardour which were at odds in the work were so violently expressed and so intensely suggested to the listener, that the tiniest musical fragment bore the imprint of this reality.

(Florestan)

(Eusebius)

Between the staves Schumann wrote: 'Here Florestan ceased, but his lips quivered with grief... Eusebius said too much about this, but his eyes sparkled with happiness.' What a distracted and confused state of affairs when it was Florestan who despaired, and Eusebius who continued to believe in a happy destiny!

Occasionally his torment gave him some respite. These were the wonderful hours which, emerging from his prostration, he would spend composing at the piano. They were also the moments spent with Chopin and Mendelssohn, whom he particularly loved and admired, and who, during the year since he had been appointed director of the Gewandhaus, had given Schumann, and the review, the support of their youthful authority. There was also the stay in June 1837, of Anna Laidlaw, the charming English pianist, to whom the *Fantasiestücke* (Op. 12) were dedicated. This dedication was a souvenir of some sentimental walks taken in the romantic surroundings of Rosenthal, and a tender and grateful reminder for a few hours of unspoiled happiness; the work contained some fleeting accents of peace, even of humour, which Schumann had forgotten long ago. 'I felt very sorry for poor Miss Laidlaw as she certainly carries you in her heart. If I were to tell you that I was jealous, I should be lying, and if I were to tell you that I wasn't, you would believe that I was lying...', Clara wrote to Robert on January 7th 1838.

Nevertheless the *Fantasiestücke* offer us one of Schumann's works that was always faithful to its nightmares, turned towards the night (*In der Nacht*), its dreams confused (*Traumeswirren*), and with the black butterflies of melancholy (*Grillen*). In this dark universe the eternal 'Why?' (*Warum?*) remained unanswered. His desperate desire for Clara again tormented him, and he recalled the sad legend of Hero and Leander, the separated lovers:

'Watch her throw herself into the sea! She calls and he answers across the waves... they are in each other's arms. But there he is, forced to set out again, and they do not succeed in separating themselves; and night returns and envelops all in its shadows...'

The long march that Robert and Clara set out on towards each other in the darkness lasted a year-and-a-half. This was a crucial period in Clara's life since up to then she had been unsure of herself and dependent upon her father. During her tours and her dull stays in Leipzig, separated from her friend, and sometimes doubtful of him, as well as being open to her father's suspicions, she became fully aware of herself and her feelings, and conscious of the secret and invincible strength which was latent in her.

When Clara at length returned to Leipzig she was in love, and she knew it. And without having seen Schumann again she gave him a public proof of her pledge: acting on her own authority, she added four of the *Études Symphoniques* to the programme she was to give on August 13th at the Gewandhaus. 'Didn't you understand that I played them because it was my only way to show you what I felt? As I was unable to do it in secret, I did it in public. Do you believe that my heart did not tremble?' How to depict his emotion at seeing her again: Clara was on the stage, applauded and fêted, Robert was among the audience; separated by the crowd and the anonymous ceremonial of a concert, they were reunited by the

alliance of their genius, their long periods of waiting and the silent surges of their feelings.

Robert, elated with happiness and hope, then wrote to Clara. It was the first of a long series of letters which they exchanged during the three years which followed. Its tone was so untroubled and confident that one forgot, as he himself must have forgotten, that in a year they might have become strangers to each other.

'Are you as loyal and strong as ever? However unassailable my faith in you, and however great my courage, what anguish is mine at knowing nothing about the one I hold to be most dear in the whole world! For that is what you are to me. Everything tells me that it *must* come to pass if we wish it and work towards it... Above all, be strong and hold firm. Do not forget to write me a "yes". I need this assurance.'

And suddenly, just as sure of herself and her sincerity, Clara pronounced the 'yes' so passionately desired. 'Is a single "yes" all you ask for? Such a little word – how important it is! Cannot a heart so full of love as mine utter it with all its soul? This is what I am doing and the word comes from my inmost depths; I say "yes" into your ear and I mean it to last for all eternity... I will prove to my father that a young heart is capable of constancy.'

*
* *

Having decided to behave in a manner which was beyond reproach, Schumann asked Wieck for the chance to have a frank discussion. The interview was 'terrible': 'Wieck was frigid and full of ill-will, and then he was confused and contradictory, and crushed you when you least expected it, and stuck a knife in your heart right up to the hilt...' Wieck's tactics were instinctively made up of contradictions, apparent reconciliations, violent leaps and blind blows of the most terrifying kind. For three years Robert's life lay at the mercy of this persecution. He was preyed upon by the impotence of his inaction, or trying to rebel, he kept on leaving and returning to Leipzig as much to disarm his torturer with his good-will as to wrest his happiness from him by force, as he had now been stripped of every illusion.

Robert gained nothing from this interview, but he left it with a fresh doubt in his mind; Wieck had succeeded in poisoning his happiness once more; would not Clara, who was used to an exciting and easy life, suffer if her existence were to become limited, difficult

Nur ein einfaches "Ja" verlangen Sie? So ein
so kleines Wörtchen — so wichtig! Doch —
sollte nicht ein Herz so voll unaussprechlicher
Liebe wie das meine, dieß kleine Wörtchen
aus ganzer Seele aussprechen können? ich
thue es und mein Innerstes flüstert es
Ihnen ewig zu.

Das Schwanken meines Herzens, die vielen
Thränen, soll ich das schildern — o nein! —
Vielleicht will es das Schicksal, daß wir
uns bald einmal sprechen und dann —
Das Vorhaben scheint mir vielleicht, doch ein
banges Herz achtet der Gefahren nicht viel.
So abermals sag ich "Ja"! Sollte
meinen achtzehnten Geburtstag zu
einem Trauertag machen? Ja nein
das wäre doch zu grausam. Auch sei ich
so lange Ihr es auch werden," nicht
die Welt soll mich irre machen, und
Ihnen werde ich zeigen daß ein Mädchen auch standhaft sein kann.
So eilig
Ihre Clara.

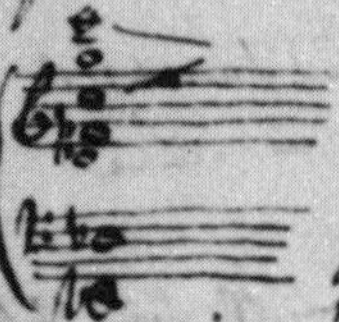

and obscure? 'Clara will secretly weep in silence', Wieck pointed out making himself an accomplice in Robert's love.

'October 4th... Yesterday I let the hours go by one after the other as I lay dreaming. Wake up! In the evening I had a lot to drink. This afternoon I tried to concentrate on my work – in vain.

'October 7th... Yesterday my spirit was again in a terrible state. So troubled, lost... where does it come from. No proper work. Bad, bad night with awful dreams. Again better in the morning.

'October 10th... The twilight is close, or the beginning of a new life.'

To Clara he wrote: 'Today I can think of nothing but you, also of your father who has shown himself to be so hard. Like you, I pass from laughter to tears. What a terrible night I have spent! How my head burned and my troubled imagination hurled me from one rock to another, ever-fearful of falling... I reproach myself for having so little confidence when, after all, I have the word of a determined and noble young girl... I am weaker than I thought.'

Nevertheless, they managed to see each other again, and the autumn twilight which descended over the Reichelsgarten was their accomplice in re-uniting them for moments which were all too brief when the joy was mingled with sorrow. 'I haven't the wish to think any more or to write about it at greater length, but while you were weeping against my breast... Clara, you made me catch a glimpse of heaven and hell.' They only came together to be separated immediately: Clara had to go off on tour and Schumann took part in her farewell concert at Leipzig, hidden in a corner 'dead and happy at the same time, tired enough to fall to the ground, and in every drop of blood, a wave of fever.'

But what was a separation when souls were in accord? From Prague and Vienna, stages on her triumphant journey, Clara would write sitting bolt upright in front of her chest-of-drawers in the evening, in her room which she had been forbidden to lock, ready to drop pen and paper furtively into a drawer if her zealous and irascible father should suddenly enter. 'My most beautiful laurels come from you', she said, thus offering him the ones she had received. And how great was her pleasure when she was responsible for the enthusiastic reception of *Carnaval* at Prague.

Carried away by their flights of fancy, Clara and Robert lived in a state of passionate ecstasy. On the night of December 31st, Schumann sat alone at his table while Clara played in Vienna. 'Come and sit next to me, put your arm round my neck, let us gaze once again into each other's eyes, without saying anything, and in a

83

state of divine happiness... Two people in the world are in love... A quarter-to has just struck, some men are singing a chorus in the distance. Do you know these two who are in love? How happy we are!' And the next day, during the first hour of the New Year: 'What a heavenly morning! All the bells are ringing, the sky is completely blue, and so pure and gilded... your letter is in front of me... to you goes my first kiss, O my soul so passionately loved!'

Clara: 'I would like to go on writing until I died of it.'

Happiness then seemed very close. Here was their house and their life: 'I see one of the rooms flooded in a dreamy twilight with flowers at the window, or the pale-blue room with the piano and the engravings... In the evening I will improvise at the piano only for you, and sometimes you will accompany me by singing in your sweet voice... and then you will fall quite happily against my heart and say to me: 'No, I never thought it would be as beautiful as this!'

'How happy I have been during these last days', Schumann wrote on February 6th, 1838, 'young and lighthearted... During the past three weeks I have composed a frightful quantity of music, jokes, stories about Egmont, family scenes with fathers, a marriage, in short, as you can see, all sorts of pleasant things! I have called it all *Novelletten*, because your name is Clara, like *la Novello*'s, and because *Wiecketten* wouldn't have sounded so well!'

And thus we have been able to avoid making a mistake: in spite of their title, these pieces were not dedicated to the beautiful singer about whom the whole of Leipzig was raving. Like everything that Schumann had written for some years, it was a secret tribute to Clara. Sprung from a single impetus, the eight *Novelletten* (Op. 21), demonstrated an almost unusual tonal relationship: five were in D major, and the rest were in neighbouring keys, all major. Was Eusebius being disowned? But in the event, he slipped into more than one page with an aura of the melancholy from which no really Schumannesque work was ever free.

The *Intermezzo* of the third *Novellette* was an evocation of the gloomy and fantastic:

> 'When shall we three meet again
> In thunder, lightning or in rain?'

were the words it bore in quotation in the edition which appeared as a musical supplement to the review. This reference to the three witches in *Macbeth* has disappeared in the modern editions and it was Alfred Cortot who recalled the sinister inspirers of this *Intermezzo* in his commentary on the work.

R. Schumann

The eighth *Novellette* was the richest of them all; it was a constant flood of ideas and forms which became entangled and worked themselves out according to a subtle rule of which Schumann alone possessed the secret. 'Music was brimming over in me', he wrote, 'I sang all the time while I was composing – and nearly everything was successful. Now I am juggling with forms...'

Clara was dazzled by the results: 'Everything in you sings so magnificently! It is true, all your heart is revealed in these beautiful melodies...' But still further marvels awaited her.

'February 12th, 1838: Composed some pretty little things: worked until Saturday on the composition of the *Kinderscenen*...

'February 24th: Composed the short piece *Träumerei*...'

To Clara: 'Is this an unconscious answer to what you wrote me one day: "Sometimes you make a childish impression on me"? If this is so, you will see that wings have sprouted on this child as I have written more than thirty pieces and have chosen a dozen of them to be collected under the title of *Kinderscenen*. You will, doubtless, find pleasure in playing them, but you will have to forget that you are a virtuoso!'

The person who had to forget that she was a virtuoso had just reached the high point of her career: while in Vienna, she had received the wonderful title of '*Kammervirtuosin*' to His Majesty, but she knew that in order to play the *Kinderscenen* (Op. 15), she would have to abandon every trace of showiness. She accepted the pieces with enthusiasm, and playing them helped to brighten the

lonely hours on her tour. Do these thirteen short pieces owe their evocative power and the feeling of poetry which suffuses them to the spontaneously childish and rudimentary language in which they are written? Of course not. The composer's maturity and his supreme mastery as a musical craftsman were revealed in every bar, and gave their unique magic to these 'retrospective views of childhood by a grown-up person.' The *Kinderscenen* are in the repertoires of all the greatest interpreters of Schumann, whose supreme artistry consists in making us forget the hours of work that went into perfecting the tiniest figure, or getting a phrase just right from the point of view of accentuation and contrast. Only instruction by these great pianists can reveal the web of problems which stretches out before the would-be interpreter of these simple evocations. Alban Berg, a modern composer whose works exceed compositions of the romantics in sheer complexity, was in agreement with them on this point. In a virulent article against certain commentators who were unable to discern the extraordinary wealth of the musical structures in *Kinderscenen*. Berg went into a deep analysis of the seventh and best-known piece in the collection, *Träumerei*. This analysis did not pretend to strip the source of Schumann's genius of its last veil, but in its surprising strictness it lit up the journeying of a melodic imagination. It restored the architecture of a four-part polyphony, and enough cannot be said of how personal this was to Schumann and unique in romantic music.

Who has not been able to discover the fact that the *Kinderscenen* contain no pianistic acrobatics to reserve them only for virtuosi, and who has not been able to penetrate into their charmed world all by himself? Not even an integral analysis in the manner of Alban Berg could describe here a development of the psychological or poetic impressions which must remain essentially subjective. But it is pleasant to remember, especially in connection with *Träumerei*, that a piece of music as human as it is popular, and whose echoes even resound in the grating voice of the barrel-organ parked down the street, can also be a polyphonic structure of a secret and fully-realised complexity; such was the paradox of Schumann's inspiration.

It was while he was still waiting that the *Kreisleriana* (Op. 16) were composed.

'May 3rd, 1838... Spent three wonderful spring days waiting for a letter. Then composed the *Kreisleriana* in four days; entirely new worlds are opening up before me...'

To Clara: 'I have noticed that my imagination is never so lively

'The picture-book' (C. Leberecht Vogel)

as when it is anxiously extended towards you. This was again the case during these last days, and while waiting for a letter from you I composed enough to fill volumes. Extraordinary music, at times mad, at times solemn and dreamy. You will open your eyes wide when you decipher it. Do you know, sometimes I have the notion that I shall finish up by bursting with music, the ideas so press and seethe within me when I dream of our love.'

'... Do you sometimes play my *Kreisleriana?* Some of the pages contain a truly savage love...'

To Simonin de Sire: 'Of all these compositions (Op. 15 to Op. 20), *Kreisleriana* is the one dearest to me. The title can only be understood by the Germans. Kreisler was a character created by E. T. A. Hoffmann; he was a strange *Kapellmeister*, a man of passion and wit. There are many things about him which should please you.'

Although the *Kreisleriana* were not a musical transcription of Hoffmann's tale, but simply a further expression of a divided and, in those years, a sorely troubled soul, it was not by accident that

A drawing by E. T. A. Hoffmann

Schumann chose as the imaginary interpreter of his inner life the character of the deluded musician, whose end so strangely foretold his own.

Together with the *Phantasie* (Op 17), the *Kreisleriana* was perhaps the finest work Schumann composed for the piano. They were both subtitled *Phantasien*, and, in its romantic meaning, the word is closer to 'nightmare' and 'hallucination' than to 'fantasy'. There was already the agitation of feverish forebodings in the very first of the eight pieces. A calmer melodic episode

followed, full of an inward quality, interrupted by two short interludes; the violence of the one, and the volatile rapidity of the other, vanished on the return of the melodic *motif*. The relentless hammer-blows provided by the rhythms of the following piece found their opposition in the peaceful harmonies of the fourth one. Then, after the changing rhythms, brought together with such violence, followed the glorious melody in the sixth piece, one of the most Schumannesque, and one of the most amazing in the whole of piano literature;

the theme of the last piece glided into it like a warning.

The desperate character which the lyrical pages of the *Kreisleriana* assumed, in the obsessive rhythm of the third, the eighth and also the seventh pieces, in which there palpitated the 'savage love' of which Schumann had spoken, revealed, in one of its key-works, what was most accomplished and most tragic in German romanticism.

Nevertheless, Schumann had within him that musical abundance from which masterpieces emerged. When Clara at last returned to Leipzig, the lovers fixed the date of their marriage for 1840, even if they had to appeal to the courts to overrule the paternal 'veto'. But Wieck, although less inclined than ever to capitulate, suddenly pretended to be prepared to give in if Schumann could give him proof of a reasonable income, and were to leave Leipzig.

Robert, ready for every concession, forbade himself to compose and dedicated himself entirely to the review. So as to fall in with Wieck's last demand, he decided to transfer the editorial to Vienna. He was prepared to sacrifice all he had: he renounced the friendly atmosphere of Leipzig and hastened his separation from Clara.

'August 1st, 1838: All day and all night, one of the most terrible in my life, I thought I was going to waste away from restlessness – it was dreadful. A good letter from Clara (she was at Dresden), the first in a fortnight, arrived in the afternoon, but this did not help me. Everything has come at once: the coming separation and the fear of being alone in a big city... Another moment of it at night and I should not have been able to stand it any more; I didn't close my eyes, so oppressed was I by frightening thoughts and the incessant sound of strange music. God preserve me from dying like this!

'October 31st, 1838: I am still incapable of working, lacking the desire, the peace and the impulse to do so. Sometimes I should like to go to sleep for entire years, then again I want to rescue myself from that and create...'

The arrival in Vienna provided a welcome diversion to his despondent state. The life there was gay and pleasant, and the Viennese themselves were affable. Schumann began to hope again and started looking for a publisher, or a position as orchestral conductor or teacher, so as to become established. But he was soon disillusioned: this incurably fickle public which had in turn applauded and booed its great musicians, which had allowed Mozart to die in misery, Beethoven in contempt, and Schubert in neglect, made its gods out of Rossini (Robert's *bête noire*) and Johann Strauss. As for the musical atmosphere, torn as it was by petty rivalries, it contained neither talent nor greatness. No one compelled recognition, and a conspiracy of mediocrity barred the way to the newcomer. Schumann very quickly gave up.

There still remained the beauty and the uplifting gaiety of the town, some concerts, and meetings with Mozart's son and Schubert's brother, who confided an unpublished symphony to him. Vienna was nothing more than a musical desert, but for someone with a receptive soul it was a desert which was still alive with marvellous murmurings. Inspired by those who had passed away, Schumann, who had not composed for months and who had not felt strong enough to do so, became aware that 'every-

The 'Wasserglacis' of Vienna

thing would return soon, and with even greater vigour than before.'

And then suddenly came the *Arabeske* (Op. 18), the *Humoreske* (Op. 20), the *Nachtstücke* (Op.23), again inspired by Hoffmann's gloomy phantasmagorias, whose discarded title *Leichenfantasie* haunted Schumann. As a reaction against this anguish came the *Faschingsschwank aus Wien* (Op. 26), the carnival pranks in Vienna, dedicated to Simonin de Sire.

Written in 1839, five years after the first *Carnaval*, this latter work did not possess the psychological complexity of its forerunner. It was a composition full of joy, colour and movement. It started with a grand *Allegro* in which the exceedingly rhythmical fast sections alternated with fragments of melody in accordance with Schumann's principle of keeping movement, attack and shading in constant opposition. Schumann had rediscovered his irreverent spirit: at the end of the *Allegro*, the '*Marseillaise*' rang out in defiance of the Imperial censor, but a dancing, carnival version of the '*Marseillaise*' in a 6/8 tempo. A tender *Romanze*, a very ironic *Scherzino*, and an agitated *Intermezzo* followed each other rapidly. And the frenzied *Finale*, with its abrupt halts and its violent accents, brought the mad burlesque of a carnival night to its climax.

It was Schumann's farewell to Vienna. For a month he lived in uncertainty as to what he should do, and soon he became restless, for Clara was in Paris, alone. Wieck, who should have accompanied her, had stayed on in Leipzig, leaving her to deal with the hazards of a journey undertaken in the middle of winter, and the difficulties of organising a tour. He counted on seeing her return soon, subdued and repentant. He did not know Clara: at Paris she chose the dates for her concerts, booked the hall, arranged and had her programmes printed, and looked after the sales of tickets. There were at that time no concert agencies, and the multiple cares which had devolved upon Wieck were in addition to his work as a piano teacher. Clara proved that she could cope with all this and so thwarted her father's imprudent calculation: 'I see', she wrote, 'that even without my father I can still continue to exist in this world.'

Schumann had not sufficient words of admiration for his 'sparkling-eyed heroine.'

'What you have just done is the most wonderful proof of your

love that you have ever given me... Ah, if I could only see you! Flames should dart from your eyes... No other young girl would have known how to stay faithful to me as you have done, for you alone are capable of loving me as you love me, and with that nobility which goes beyond words. I can tell you nothing more; it would need you to be able to catch sight of me during my consecrated hours, to see me dreaming, when I am dreaming of you...'

But the evil angel of this love was still to trouble him: Wieck had not reached the end of his resources, and having proved himself incapable of bringing his daughter to heel, he appealed to her tenderness in such a heart-rending manner that Clara, formerly so firm, gave in to this sentimental blackmail. She asked Robert again to put off going to the courts for justice, as they had both decided to do. For him this was a mortal blow. Month after month, and year after year, he had been dragged lower and lower and struck at with ever increasing force. But this time the blow came from Clara herself, and his resistance was at an end: the month of May 1839 was laden with bitterness, desperate temptations and presentiments of death. Schumann, already sorely tried by the sudden death of his brother Ernest, dreamed of breaking things off and so snatching himself from this endless struggle and this tireless grief; his absolute confidence in Clara's love was suddenly diminished and he was again beset by his obsession with suicide.

At last, faced with Clara's undertaking not to seek a further postponement, Schumann yielded; but he remained shattered by all that had gone before.

'It was your second letter which hurt me most of all; if you reread it later on you will be pained to believe that you could have written it. Everything happened at the same time. Your father again declared himself against me in the most insulting fashion... and on top of that I received you second letter, as cold as the grave, so discontented and obstinate. I went through terrible days. Such emotions affect me down to the smallest fibres of my being. Where you are concerned, my reactions are tenfold; I remained stricken to my very marrow, I doubted you and asked myself if your heart had changed towards me. I opened your last letter trembling, I read, and I went on reading; it seemed that the gates of heaven were opening before me, one after the other. I had found you again...'

To a final attempt, the intractable father gave as his answer that 'Wieck did not wish to have any connection with Schumann.' Clara then stopped dreaming of an impossible reconciliation between her love and her affection as a daughter, and signed, together with Schumann, the request asking the Tribunal to authorise their marriage (July 16th, 1839). On her return from Paris she sought refuge in Berlin with her mother, who had long been divorced from Wieck, and was very happy to give her daughter the blessing which he had refused her.

'Today', wrote Schumann in June, 'I enter my twenty-ninth year; the greater part of my life is doubtless behind me. I shall not live to be very old, I know that with certainty: what I have had to undergo on your account, my great sufferings, have torn me to shreds. But it is you who will still bring healing and peace to me.'

And now should have come the brightest hours of the year 1839, 'the one most weighed-down with sufferings, but also the richest in joys.' However, in spite of the certainty that happiness was close at hand, Schumann 'tired to death, stupefied by grief', felt all his life dried-up in him: 'I have no reason for gaiety and I am often silent for days on end without thinking of anything and without doing anything except mumbling to myself.' Clara's presence and the nearness of the happy outcome would sometimes draw him from his sadness; but his sterile prostration lasted for months. Right up to February 1840 the composer who had written two years earlier: 'Never again will music be silent in me', remained completely silent.

Wieck, in the meantime, blinded by his impotent jealousy, lost all sense of restraint. He made exorbitant financial claims, became the patron of Camille Pleyel, a young virtuoso rival of his daughter, and did his best to hinder the legal proceedings. At the second hearing of the case on December 18th, 1839, he insulted Schumann with such vehemence that the presiding judge had repeatedly to make him take back what he had said. He cast doubts upon the young man's heredity and mental balance (his only sister had died insane at a very early age); he made use of extravagant calumnies and ended up by accusing him of inveterate drunkenness. This time he had gone too far, and Schumann sued him for defamation of character. But the decision of the case was postponed until the summer.

With life torn between constant struggle and divinely happy moments spent with Clara, Schumann, no longer able to resist, finally escaped into the world of creation. 'At the moment I am writing a lot of music, as I always do in the month of February' he wrote to Clara who had gone off again on tour. 'You are going to be astonished by all I have written during your absence – they are not pieces for piano, but I don't want to tell you as yet what they are...' The mystery was revealed, they were his first *lieder*, the *Liederkreis* (Op. 24), setting of poems by Heine: 'Since yesterday morning I have written twenty-seven pages of music of which all I can tell you is that, while composing them, I was laughing and crying with joy... Farewell, my Clara! Sounds and music are killing me at this moment and I feel that I could die of them. Ah, Clara, what divine happiness there is in writing for the voice! I have been deprived of it too long.'

While in the ecstasy of his creation, Schumann suddenly freed himself from his inner prison and dominated the conflicts and awful contradictions of his life. The Schumann who had been stupefied and prostrated by grief, revived so as to utter his immortal cry: 'I would like to sing like the nightingale, and die of it.' Instead, he lived by it. It was an uninterrupted flow – more than a hundred and thirty songs were written in 1840 – in which Schumann found salvation at the same time as the supreme fulfilment of his art. The piano now seemed too narrow for him; the *lied* offered him the struggle and the agreement between the instrument and the voice, the union of poetry and music, and the magic of song by which man spontaneously became music.

The reunion between Robert and Clara took place in Berlin in April 1840, and Schumann had the additional pleasure of hearing Mendelssohn sing his first song, accompanied at the piano by Clara. On his return, still joyful, he composed the *Liederkreis* (Op. 39), with

QUOD
FELIX FAUSTUMQUE ESSE IUBEAT
SUMMUM NUMEN
AUCTORITATE
HUIC LITTERARUM UNIVERSITATI
AB

FERDINANDO I
IMPERATORE ROMANO GERMANICO
ANNO MDLVII CONCESSA
CLEMENTISSIMIS AUSPICIIS
SERENISSIMORUM
MAGNI DUCIS ET DUCUM SAXONIAE
NUTRITORUM ACADEMIAE IENENSIS
MUNIFICENTISSIMORUM
RECTORE ACADEMIAE MAGNIFICENTISSIMO
AUGUSTO ET POTENTISSIMO PRINCIPE AC DOMINO

CAROLO FRIDERICO
MAGNO DUCE SAXONIAE VIMARIENSIUM ATQUE ISENACENSIUM PRINCIPE LANDGRAVIO THURINGIAE
MARCHIONE MISNIAE PRINCIPALI DIGNITATE COMITE HENNEBERGAE
DYNASTA BLANKENHAYNII NEOSTADII AC TAUTENBURGI
PRORECTORE ACADEMIAE MAGNIFICO
VIRO PERILLUSTRI ATQUE EXCELLENTISSIMO

FERDINANDO HANDIO
PHILOSOPHIAE DOCTORE ARTIUMQUE LIBERALIUM MAGISTRO
MAGNI DUCIS SAXONIAE VIMARIENSIS ET ISENACENSIS A CONSILIIS AULAE INTIMIS GRAECARUM LITTERARUM PROFESSORE PUBLICO ORDINARIO
SEMINARII PHILOLOGICI DIRECTORE ACADEMIAE IMPERIALIS PETROPOLITANAE SOCIO AC SOCIETATIS GANDAVIENSIS LATINAE SODALI
MINERALOGICARUM PETROPOLITANARUM ET JENENSIS SODALI
DECANO ORDINIS PHILOSOPHORUM ET BRABEUTA
MAXIME SPECTABILI
VIRO PERILLUSTRI ATQUE AMPLISSIMO

ERNESTO REINHOLDO
PHILOSOPHIAE DOCTORE ARTIUMQUE LIBERALIUM MAGISTRO
MAGNI DUCIS SAXONIAE VIMARIENSIS ET ISENACENSIS A CONSILIIS PHILOSOPHIAE PROFESSORE PUBLICO ORDINARIO
ORDO PHILOSOPHORUM
VIRO PRAENOBILISSIMO ATQUE DOCTISSIMO

ROBERTO SCHUMANN
ZWICKAVIENSI
COMPLURIUM SOCIETATUM MUSICARUM SODALI
QUI RERUM MUSIS SACRARUM ET ARTIFEX INGENIOSUS ET IUDEX ELEGANS MODIS HUMORI TUM SCITE COMPONENDIS
TUM DOCTE IUDICANDO ATQUE PRAECEPTIS DE SENSU PULCHRITUDINIS VENUSTATISQUE
OPTIMIS EDENDIS MAGNAM NOMINIS FAMAM ADEPTUS EST

DOCTORIS PHILOSOPHIAE HONORES
DIGNITATEM IURA ET PRIVILEGIA
INGENII DOCTRINAE ET VIRTUTIS SPECTATAE INSIGNIA ATQUE ORNAMENTA
DETULIT
DELATA
PUBLICO HOC DIPLOMATE
CUI IMPRESSUM EST SIGNUM ORDINIS PHILOSOPHORUM

95

Schumann's diploma from the University of Jena

words by Eichendorff, and the *Dichterliebe* (Op. 48), to texts again by Heine. 'No one alive is as gifted as you', cried Clara, 'my growing love and admiration for you can hardly keep pace with each other.'

At a new hearing of the Tribunal, Schumann set great store by the honorary title of Doctor of Philosophy which the University of Jena had just awarded him in the most flattering terms (he had quite frankly solicited this mark of middle-class respectability by using a friend as intermediary); numerous testimonies, that of Mendelssohn in particular, were presented in his favour, and refuted Wieck's slanders. Wieck himself was sentenced to twelve days in prison for his 'shameless accusation' that Schumann was a drunkard, and on August 1st the tribunal passed its judgment authorising the marriage.

'When we are at the altar, I believe that the word "yes" will never have been pronounced with a more burning faith in a happy future.' This word was pronounced by Clara and Schumann on September 12th, 1840, in a small village church at Schönefeld, near Leipzig.

'A myrtle from my bridal garland' (Clara)

96

To Die of Singing

The German romantic poets very often went to popular poetry for their inspiration and so perpetuated its themes and forms. The musicians also knew how to find their way back to the sources: it was the *Volkslied*, the folk-song, which gave birth to the romantic *lied;* the passage from one to the other was spontaneous and imperceptible and the frontier between them remained shadowy and undefined.

Sprung from a common source, poetry and music passionately sought to become united in romanticism, and so reached, in a more confused state than they had ever been, 'that vast domain beyond the boundaries of language.' This ambition made it necessary for the *lied* to go beyond the over-narrow margins of its earliest models. It was towards the end of the eighteenth century that it gradually freed itself from the popular strophic form, which it found too stiff and rigid, and therefore insufficiently expressive. When it became necessary for the romantic song to provide its own strict rules, it found that it could maintain flexibility by introducing melodic variations from one verse to another.

But a form of declamation, which grew freer all the time, soon took over and was able to express the most delicate shades of feeling and psychological complexities which sometimes took on a truly dramatic form. Beethoven had already made use of a purely dramatic form of declamation in 'In questa tomba oscura' and in his song-cycle, *An die ferne Geliebte.*

Weber, who had written over a hundred songs, Zumsteeg and Karl Loewe, whose famous ballads Schumann thought highly of, had contributed to this development. But it was Schubert who, setting the mark of genius upon this still changing form, had brought about the mature and definitive blossoming of its greatness. The *lied* became a complex and profound piece of music, a dramatic microcosm. It was, therefore, a perfect art form when Schumann discovered it, but he managed to bring it to a still higher stage of perfection.

Schumann had enriched his musical inspiration with all his human and literary experience. Extremely well-acquainted with the artistic and aesthetic currents of his time, he dominated them by the force of his intelligence. His joys and his very sufferings, which affected him so deeply, equipped him to perceive and to represent their echoes with greater variety, shade, and depth. His extensive culture had been enlivened by his personal experience as a writer, by his adolescent attempts, and by the poetical as well as the critical view he had of his role as a combatant musician. The extreme diversity of his nature made him respond to the appeal of a great variety of forms of genius and inspiration; he was able to rediscover himself in them, while at the same time remaining himself.

To this richness in similarities in Schumann, corresponded an extraordinary diversity of ways of writing, an extreme mastery and freedom in this handling of constantly new forms, always adapted to the rhythms of the text and its affective tonality, and always unique.

The piano was too intimate an expression of Schumann's ego not to be, when placed close to the voice and on its identical level, 'another character' who conversed with it and sometimes even absorbed and dominated it. This unity of voice and piano, both as independent and as necessary to one another in dialogue as in dramatic conflict, was essentially Schumannesque. The long prelude which gave rise to the voice, and the long postlude in which it disappeared, were quite new in the field of the *lied*, and delineated the contours of this perfected romantic universe.

And so Schumann brought about this intimate union between poetry and music which had always been dreamed of. German romantic poems had been intended from the first for a musical destiny: those by Rückert and Eichendorff called for melody, and seemed incomplete without it. Not only did it give them a richer resonance, but their structure and form seemed to prescribe this alliance.

100

In his 248 songs, Schumann called on nearly all the poets of his time, from the most famous to the most obscure. A real and many-sided romantic, Schumann found in them all the themes which were dear to him; but deeper and more imponderable similarities, which are too often passed over in silence, appealed to him as a song-writer. It was, even beyond the poem's actual meaning, through its words, its rhythm, its structure, its general sense of movement and everything which constituted its poetic individuality, that a poem challenged the composer who found, by a direct, and almost sensual contact, the incitement to find the harmonies for it, and like the foreshadowing of an agreement possible between poet and musician. This spontaneous contact between created and uncreated forms was an important determining factor for Schumann: it was thus that his inspiration responded directly to the poetry of Heine and Eichendorff. A lesser affinity of style had the possible result that he borrowed relatively little from Goethe, in spite of his great admiration for him and the richness of his romantic themes.

As early as his first *lieder*, Schumann's poetic horizon appeared in all its fullness. In addition, he did not limit himself to the German romantics, and his first work for the voice was not, as is generally thought, the *Liederkreis* (Op. 24) based on poems by Heine, but the *Schlusslied des Narren* from Shakespeare's *Twelfth Night;* this dated from February 1st, 1840 and not from 1851. This was Shakespeare's only appearance in Schumann's songs, but the composer was not unaffected by the fact that it was through the poet of his childhood that he had penetrated into the world of the *lied*.

In *Myrthen* (Op. 25), three English poets were added to the list headed by Shakespeare. Robert Burns had beguiled Schumann with the candour of his popular inspiration, and the simplicity and the purity of his verse ('My heart is in the Highlands'). Thomas Moore provided him with two Venetian songs whose flexible rhythms evoked, in triple counterpoint, the fall of the oar, the rocking of the gondola and the song of the gondolier. But it was Byron who was the closest to him, and in *Myrthen*,

Robert Burns

a 'Hebrew Melody', *Mein Herz ist schwer*, revealed the similarity between the two geniuses. It was followed much later by the *Drei Gesänge* (Op. 45), and by the dramatic scenes from *Manfred*.

But it was in the treasury of German romantic poetry, from Rückert to Heine, and Goethe to Mörike, that Schumann found most of his material. Out of thirty poets, Rückert, Eichendorff and Heine, most of all, were his most beloved inspirers.

Rückert

It fell to Rückert to open the *Myrthen* song-cycle with *Widmung* ('Dedication'), when it was this garland of myrtles with which Schumann's finally triumphant love would crown his betrothed. The two songs of the betrothed, *Zum Schluss* ('The Last Word') and *Widmung* were the most ardent and intimate of the songs which Schumann offered to Clara. Rückert was also the poet of their overflowing happiness, and it was together that they wrote *Liebesfrühling* (Op. 27). The six *lieder* which comprised the *Minnespiel* (Op. 101), themselves excerpts from Rückert's *Liebesfrühling*, reflected the joy of their love: a man's voice alternated with a woman's, Clara and Schumann sung of the ecstasy of happy lovers.

102

Schumann loved Rückert for his mastery of verse and poetic rhythm and also, despite his erudition, for keeping so close to the strictness and simplicity of popular forms. He turned him into his love-poet and wished to ignore the other Rückert, the poet who, while using the same almost naïve and sometimes playful tone, wrote songs about madness and death: the author of the *Kindertotenlieder*.

Eichendorff

In the works of Eichendorff, Schumann rediscovered nature, which had always been one of his most powerful inspirations. His poetry,

which also derived from the folksong, displayed an unusual power and purity in its use of traditional forms. He evoked the mysterious forests of Silesia, among the most enchanting sights of nature; he was a '*Wanderer*', an inspired vagabond who listened and responded to the voices of distant marvels.

'In nature, in the dreams of the solitude of forests, as in the labyrinth of the human heart, a wonderful and everlasting song has slumbered since the beginning, a bewitched beauty which it is reserved for the poet to deliver.'

It was in these words that Eichendorff defined his poetic destiny, and his 'wonderful song' was the same as Schumann's. A creative affinity has seldom been as strong and as happy as in the twelve songs which made up the *Liederkreis* (Op. 39). With what delicacy the prelude of *Zwielicht* evoked the atmosphere of the descending dusk, and the forest quietly taking

Eichendorff (drawing by F. Kugler)

'The dance of spring' (Hans Thoma)

on the life which only the poet was allowed to see in movement.
The voice whispered in a confidential tone:

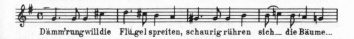

Dämm'rung will die Flügel spreiten, schaurig rühren sich die Bäume...

it was the most discreet accent in Schumann's songs; the song
entwined around the voices of the piano so as to weave impalpable
webs of sound. The *lieder* in this cycle, *Schöne Frunde, Die Stille,
Mondnacht* and *Frühlingsnacht* are among Schumann's most de-
servedly famous. In *Mondnacht*, night full of promises, the poet's
thought, set free, made off towards its own country. The short
piano introduction was transformed in an uninterrupted succession
of sustained chords over which the voice hovered. Imperceptibly
the harmonies changed and seemed to melt into each other. All
seemed unreal and timeless...

Heine

It was in Heine that Schumann rediscovered himself most fully, and found displayed all the opposed tendencies of his nature. For Heine was also a split personality: the irreconcilable combination of a romantically pure heart and a destructive irony had fascinated Schumann, who was himself far from being a person to exercise this disillusioned and sometimes grating irony, or to make cruel parodies of the heart's most fervent enthusiasms. Although sometimes sharp, Schumann's irony was only the weapon of a conviction, never of a doubt. It differed from Heine's in that it never marred the purity of a movement that was spontaneous and profound. Any encounter between the two men on a level other than poetical was impossible. When Schumann, as a youthful truant from school and an enthusiast of his poetry, had met Heine in Munich, he had been shocked by the trembling poet's attitude of indifferent elegance. Wishing to overcome this early disillusion, as soon as he had composed the *Liederkreis* (Op. 24), Schumann sent them to his inspirer.

'In writing these lines I am satisfying an old and lasting desire to get a little closer to you, for I am sure that you must have forgotten the visit which I paid you in Munich a good many years ago when I was very young indeed. May you be pleased by the music I have composed to your *lieder*! If my powers only equalled the passion with which I wrote it, you would have good grounds for feeling hopeful. Would you like my friend Stephen Heller to give you an opportunity of hearing these songs? A word from you saying that they had been well-received would fill me with joy.'

Schumann never had that joy, and the forgetful Heine complained three years later that he had not received a single one of the songs which had been composed in Germany to his poems.

But the poet and the musician had met on a plane beyond that which separated them. Heine had given thirty-eight of his poems to Schumann who found in them, together with an echo of his contradictions and his changing moods, the attraction of a music which responded mysteriously to his own, and which became one with it in an almost physical sense.

All too rarely performed, the *Liederkreis* (Op. 24) allows us to follow Schumann's first footsteps in his new musical world. He moved forward in it as though dazzled, almost gropingly to begin with, gradually uncovering the secrets of that wonderful world, and asserting a truly personal style as early as in the third song *Ich wandelte unter den Bäumen*. The song began with a prelude rich in

106

polyphony, and with the curve of the first vocal phrase was revealed that convergence of the voice and the piano, equal but independent, which is the hall-mark of Schumann's *lieder*. In *Warte, warte, wilder Schiffsmann* he made full use of his dramatic sense of contrast and accent, and an echo of this song of farewell persisted, groaning, into its long postlude. In the last song of the cycle, *Mit Myrthen und Rosen*, Schumann grappled with a larger and already complex form which he mastered thoroughly: the vocal compass was wide, a strong breath was needed and the voice led the piano, which resumed the opening rhythm of the cycle in a long postlude, thus affirming its unity.

If the *Liederkreis* already represented success, the famous cycle *Dichterliebe* (Op. 48), which resulted from the same creative urge of 1840, was a total achievement. It comprised 16 songs, unique in their astonishing diversity of inspiration, composition and *'stimmung'* ('atmosphere' would be the rough equivalent for this untranslatable key-term of romanticism).

In the first song, *Im wunderschönen Monat Mai*, the voice blossomed forth freely while the piano tirelessly repeated the same rhythmical figure. Short, fleeting, and sung *mezza-voce*, the third song, *Die Rose, die Lilie* revolved around a single, simple *motif*, disappearing as soon as it had drawn us into its game of sounds . . .

Ich grolle nicht is one of Schumann's most completely romantic songs which imparted to Heine's text, itself hovering on the brink of irony, a feeling that was dramatic in the extreme. The voice's

striving towards the high notes had a passionate accent which was lent a sombre colouring by the deep bass notes of the piano. This feeling of a vast expanse of sound disappeared in the following song, *Und wüssten's die Blumen* (No. 8), and was reduced to a halo of light. The music was without depth of register, as if without roots, a continuous rustling, a transparency where the murmuring voice afforded the only perceptible outline.

There was still further innovation in *Das ist ein Flöten und Geigen*. Independent of the voice, the piano developed a full-scale melodic line which crossed and re-crossed the vocal part and only rejoined it at the conclusion; a dance-rhythm, quite self-contained but inseparable from the whole, formed part of the interplay between instrument and voice.

Schumann had conveyed all the bitter-sweet irony of *Ein Jüngling liebt ein Mädchen* ('A youth loved a maiden'), one of Heine's most celebrated poems: the piano seemed to laugh at the voice's emotion, and contradicted it incessantly in accents that were off the beat. The last song of the *Dichterliebe*, *Die alten, bösen Lieder* ('The bad old songs'), derived from an entirely different kind of inspiration.

Its deep register attracted the voice like a lover, and all the melodic lines converged towards it. A strange modulation marked the finish of the vocal part, the piano developed a long postlude in which a new melody, immediately intermingled with some long sustained notes, was stated, blossomed out and rose up, only to sink down again on a deep chord.

It was in the inexhaustible collection called *Myrthen* (Op. 25), which has already been mentioned, that the famous *Du bist eine Blume* ('You are like a flower') as well as *Die Lotosblume*, a calm and motionless melody with fluid and changing harmonies, were to be found. Other Heine-Schumann masterpieces were scattered in the collections of *Romanzen und Balladen* (Opp. 45, 49, 53) and included

'The night patrol' (Karl Spitzweg)

Die feindlichen Brüder and *Die Beiden Grenadiere* which contained an echo of the 'Marseillaise'; it was, finally, in the triptych from Op. 53, *Der arme Peter*, that the poet and the musician responded with subtle refinement to a naïvely popular inspiration. Nowhere had the union of a supreme art and the most spontaneous song of a nation attained this degree of intimacy and success. Heine had drawn this macabre rondeau, where the cruelty was softened, out of the rigid and rhythmical popular German couplet form in which so many nameless authors had sung their lullabies of death, and danced to little funereal waltzes. Schumann grasped his intention immediately: two chords like the bagpipes, and there was 'Poor Peter' preparing to commit suicide because of love to a dancing rhythm in ¾ time, while the piano developed some exquisite

111

polyphony! But in the third song, the voice abandoned this *ritornello* which had kept on revolving around itself, and while the poem continued on a playful note:

> 'He has lost his dearest treasure
> How can he still love and live?'

the voice rose very high in an immense trajectory of torment and shattered on the final cadence where a funeral drum resounded on the piano.

It was again Heine who, in 1852, inspired Schumann with his last song, *Mein Wagen rollet langsam* ('Slowly rolls my waggon'), in his Op. 142, a strange song whose prelude drew out its jolting rhythms in deeper and deeper registers. So as to compensate for this, the melodic line was long and peaceful. The poet lay dreaming... suddenly two mocking phantoms appeared, whirled around him, entwined and vanished... The voice grew silent, only the piano pursued the poet's thoughts, remained for some time in a dreaming state, and then, taking up the lullaby-rhythm of the opening, disappeared.

Goethe

If Goethe did not occupy as privileged a position in Schumann's vocal output as in Schubert's, it could not be said that he had not been properly appreciated by a musician who was hardly exclusive, and extremely diverse in his poetical affinities. When one thinks of the *Requiem für Mignon* for solo voices, chorus and orchestra, as well as the enormous *Faust* which haunted the composer from 1844 until the time of his death, then Goethe's place is assured in Schumann's work by reason of his pre-eminence above the entire romantic Parnassus. As a *lieder*-writer, Schumann was inspired by eighteen of his poems which are to be found scattered in several collections. Starting with *Myrthen*, there were the three poems taken from the *Westöstlicher Diwan: Freisinn, Talismane* and *Lieder der Zuleika*, and in the Op. 51, a very beautiful *Liebeslied*, calm and serene, and sustained by the deep sonorities of the piano. But it was in the cycle of poems taken from *Wilhelm Meister*, for which Schumann had a particular affection, that the inspirations of both men met most happily. In the *Ballade des Harfners*, the piano, closely blended with the voice, observed the smallest poetic inflexions of the text; in *Wer nie sein Brot mit Tränen ass* ('Who never ate his bread in sorrow') it assumed a pictorial role, an almost 'impressionist' character.

112

Kerner

The *Zwölf Lieder* of Op. 35, taken from Kerner, showed that the musician thought less of psychological agreement than he did of the affinities between poetical structures. Not a single one of Kerner's poems which Schumann set to music during the early months of his marriage, when his well-being was assured by his happiness in love, reflected either joy or peace. *Stirb Lieb, und Freud* ('Joy and love, all dead'), *Sehnsucht* ('The traveller's farewell'), *Auf das Trinkglas eines verstorbenen freundes* ('To a dead friend'), *Stille Tränen* ('Secret tears'), were all songs weighed down with sadness, solitude and renunciation. In addition, there was nothing dramatic about them: the expression was altogether inward and contemplative. When the voice wanted to take wing towards a livelier part, to answer a call of nature, as of a bursting storm, an abrupt discouragement thwarted its urge and recalled a misfortune without remedy.

Lenau

Two song-cycles were taken from texts by Lenau whose destiny strangely recalls that of Schumann: at the age of forty-six, the gloomy poet gave way to a mental disorder from which only death could deliver him. More than the *Vier Hussaren lieder* ('Four songs of Hussards', Op. 117), the *Sechs Gedichte* (Op. 90) were masterpieces with a very personal tone. *Der Schwere Abend* ('Evening of anguish'), whose knell-like rhythm gave rise to a deep musical resonance, is one of Schumann's finest songs. In the dark tonality of E flat minor a song arose with a strange rhythm which was suddenly interrupted in the middle of its development by a violent chord of the seventh. Everything remained suspended, then the song started once more and reached the lowest notes of its compass. The postlude was a *crescendo* of monumental chords, but it was on the most lightly touched harmony that the *lied* ended.

Geibel, Mörike, and a whole cohort of lesser-known poets — Mosen, author of the well-known *Der Nussbaum* ('The Walnut-tree'), Pfarrius, Strachwitz inspired Schumann to compose some admirable *lieder*. To Geibel we owe the two Spanish cycles: *Spanisches Liederspiel* (Op. 74) and the *Spanische Liebeslieder* (Op. 138), as well as *Sehnsucht*, whose fiery and passionate melody opened and concluded on the piano, on the crest of an immense wave of sound, and in a truly impressionistic manner which had nothing in common with the role of accompaniment formerly entrusted to the instrument.

'Melancholy' (C. D. Friedrich)

Chamisso

It was Chamisso, author of *Peter Schlemihl*, the man who lost his shadow, who provided Schumann with the poems for his *Frauenliebe und Leben* ('A woman's love and life', Op. 42), one of his most famous cycles. Was it the chastely amorous atmosphere of these short poems, or the extreme simplicity of their forms and rhythms which made him surrender to their charm only a few months before his marriage to Clara? In any case, what he made out of them provided a striking disposal of the old belief according to which a song was only a musical commentary and a translation of the sentiments expressed in the poem. In this case the beauty of the *lied* would depend upon that of the poetic text. Now, all musicians have sometimes set deficient texts to music, and *Frauenliebe und Leben*, one of Schumann's most immortal works, had no common measure with the text but absorbed it completely, and left only a play of sounds with the metre of verses such as the following:

'Happiness is love, love is happiness,
I have said it and will never take it back...
... Only a mother knows what it is to love and be happy,
Oh, how I pity the man who cannot feel a mother's happiness...'

These rather foolish poems provided the musician only with a theme, an emotional atmosphere to serve as a starting point for the free flight of his musical imagination; the music revealed its own poem, and substituted its unique and ineffable feeling for that of the text. Contrasting forms of great diversity alternated; the long postlude took up the theme of the first song according to a procedure which was dear to Schumann, thus affirming the unity of this superb cycle.

Chamisso, too, inspired *Die Löwenbraut* ('The lion's bride'), a gloomy tale about a lion, a young girl and her lover armed with a long rifle, which ended in bloodshed. Also by Chamisso were *Die Kartenlegerin* and *Die rote Hanne* (after Béranger) which comprised the *Drei Gesänge* (Op. 31) which recalled the style of Loewe's ballads: their musical phrases were long and winding, moulded by frequent modulations and rhythmic changes.

116

Elisabeth Kulmann, Mary Stuart

Elisabeth Kulmann, a young poetess who died at the age of seventeen, was one of these kindred spirits whom Schumann loved invoking. He pledged an admiration to her which to us seems scarcely merited by her works. But the unforced and mystical accent of her song seemed to Schumann to belong to the voice of a prophet.

It was due to her inspiration that he composed the *Sieben Lieder* (Op. 104), all very short and simple. *Du nennst mich armes Mädchen* ('You call me a poor girl') was one of the most beautiful. 'It happened,' Schumann explained to us, 'that thoughtless children jeered at her because of her poverty; this song was an answer to their mockery...' In it he managed to convey a soft melancholy which was accentuated by the use of the interval of the augmented fourth. In *Die letzten Blumen starben* ('Last flowers, you are dying') the funereal premonition of Schumann and the young poetess met. *Gekämpft hat meine Barke* ('My boat has struggled') concluded this contemplative homage.

Yet another tragic destiny inspired the cycle of *Gedichte der Königin Maria Stuart* (Op. 135), five *lieder* to the poems by the unfortunate Queen of Scotland. The music was not obedient to the 'vow of poverty' imposed on the songs of Op. 104, but in it the grief attained something of the grandiose; the piano kept in the background so as to let the melody be displayed fully; from the very first entry of the voice in the *Abschied von Frankreich* ('Farewell to France')

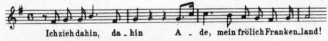

Ich zieh dahin, da – hin A – de, mein frölich Franken land!

the pathetic beauty of the little-known cycle was in full evidence.

Nach der Geburt ihres Sohnes ('After the birth of her son') was a prayer to Christ to safeguard her son. It was harmonised like a chorale; the voice almost motionless, intoned, and a heavy cadence marked the final 'Amen'. *An die Königin Elisabeth* ('To Queen Elizabeth') was a breathless melody, abrupt and angular and with strained rhythms. The piano followed close after the voice's poignant declamation. The *Abschied von der Welt* ('Farewell to the *World*') and *Gebet* ('Prayer'), came last. In the final one, the economy of the writing conveyed a feeling of inexorable fatality. It was one of Schumann's masterpieces out of so many bequeathed to us in that ecstasy which made him cry out: 'I should like to die of singing...'

118

Schumann's house at Leipzig

I am tempted to smash my piano

'Few events, much happiness', thus began the diary of their marriage which Robert and Clara kept in turn for three years. Was Schumann going to abdicate the restlessness of his youth? At length appeased, was he going to repudiate the romantic torments which had inspired so many of his masterpieces? Were Eusebius and Florestan finally to be reconciled. No, but his adventure would, henceforth, take place entirely within him, whilst his social life unwound, modestly and painstakingly, in the bosom of a united family, similar in appearance to that of a good German middle-class household of the time.

Thanks to his daily notes – the intimate journal was a habit of the period, sometimes carried to the point of madness – we are able to follow the life of a romantic musician, so different from the existence of composers of the preceding century. In the eighteenth century, even if they were not attached to princes, wearing livery like Haydn and the young Mozart, they would gravitate towards the courts, living, for the most part, on bounties dispensed to them by the great. At the beginning of the nineteenth century the courts were less numerous and less sumptuous. A middle-class public had formed and concerts had become more frequent. The era of virtuosi, independent and superb wanderers, had been born. Liszt had not owed his fame to the favour of princes but to that of a public which was constantly on the increase. It was in the same state of independence of all wealthy patronage that Schumann exercised his art. He sold his works to his publisher, and it was from his position as editor of a review, and later as conductor of an orchestra, that he demanded his sustenance as well as a certain social dignity which he valued highly.

The relationship between Clara and Schumann was a perfect one, not only in love, but in art, and in the aspirations of the two artists who had pledged a reciprocal admiration, and who respected in each other the needs of their vocations. 'The perfection of her playing has made me forget the woman for the artist,' Robert wrote in their diary; and Clara: 'My veneration for his genius, his intelligence for the composer that he is, grows with every work...'

From the early weeks of their marriage, Robert began to form, according to his ideal, his wife's taste and culture which had rather suffered from being subjected to the exclusive education of a child prodigy. Clara had read practically nothing. He initiated her to Byron, Shakespeare and, of course, to 'his unique' Jean-Paul. Victor Hugo pleased her less: 'Frivolities, vulgarities, incoherence, improbability' was what she thought of *Notre-Dame de Paris*. 'This kind of work is intended especially for Frenchmen who love only the horrible and the discordant; such a work is an abomination to a healthy German nature.'

Although brought up in the cult of Mozart and Beethoven, Clara had a predilection for the Italians which went against Schumann's convictions, and she also remained attached to the champions of virtuosity who offered the pianists nothing but successful acrobatics. Her tastes altered: Robert made her study the symphonies of Beethoven and the fugues of Bach, and she, who admired the B minor Mass but saw nothing in the *Chromatic Fantasia* but a 'chaos of passages which gave her no musical enjoyment,' played it marvellously later on. By deepening and enriching her musical understanding, Schumann found in Clara, who expected much of him but kept all her independence, an increasingly productive rivalry.

'I have completed a short song-cycle to poems by Kerner,' Robert wrote in October 1840. 'Clara has had pleasure from them and also pain, for often, as the price of my *lieder*, she has had to put up with my silences and absences.' She put up with them patiently although she came to grieve over the 'coldness' which Robert had shown towards her, absorbed, as he was, in the composition of his First Symphony. The sacrifice which Clara had to make of her art and her career was even heavier. The household had only one piano, and when Schumann was composing Clara had to remain in the

122

background; sometimes she was unable to play for several days and the diary reflected her restlessness, her fears of retrogression and Schumann's scruples. She remembered her tours with nostalgia, and wanted to use her art to replace the lucrative tasks which tore Robert from his creation. 'The thought that you have to work so as to earn money is odious to me... I should like to do something so as to ensure that your existence is completely dedicated to art. I experience profound suffering every time I have to ask you for money, and you give me what you have earned. It often seems to me that this is driving all the poetry out of your life.'

Sometimes Clara could put up with it no longer and would not stop until she had gone off on tour. She felt the need to be prodigal with her talent, which was in full flower, and she could not do without the applause with which she had lived since her childhood. In February 1842, six months after the birth of her first child, she started on her way. Schumann accompanied her from concert to concert until they reached Hamburg, where he said goodbye to her: Clara went on to conquer Copenhagen, where she remained for two months.

An extract from the diary for March 1842 reads: 'One of the most foolish things I have ever done was to allow you to go far away from me!, and I realise it more and more. May God bring you happily back to me! While waiting, I shall watch over our little daughter. Separation has made me feel yet again the unusual anomaly of our situation. Ought I to neglect my talent so as to act as your chaperon on the journey? And you, on your side, ought you not to make use of your own talent because I am tied to my review and my piano? We have found a solution: you take a travelling companion and I return to my work to be near our child.

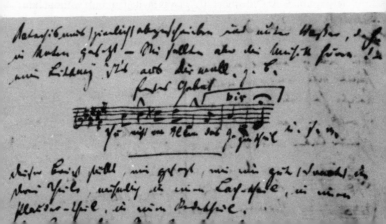

Bremen

'But what will the world say? These are the thoughts which torment me. We must find a means of assuring the parallel development of our two talents. I dream of America. Frightening decision!'

In fact he did dream of it one morning when he was feeling particularly vigorous and found himself at Bremen, the port for long voyages. With Clara, he weighed the pros and the cons; but a magazine happened to come into their hands containing a poem which they read, and which 'made them feel very sad': it had to do with a young man who had left for distant lands and who, disappointed in his hopes, threw himself into the sea together with his lyre. This portent left them in a thoughtful mood.

Schumann never ceased to detest these tours. If he accompanied Clara, he had all too often the humiliating impression that most people thought of him simply as the husband of the famous pianist. This was because his name and his genius remained unknown to a large public. At Oldenburg, Clara was invited to court without him; later on, at Vienna and again in Holland, 'illustrious personages', to whom he was presented, asked him if he was 'also a musician'.

If he stayed in Leipzig during Clara's absence, 'the house seemed silent and as if dead... For it is pleasant to live with a sweet and loving wife. Truly my next symphony should be called 'Clara', and I shall paint her with flutes, oboes and harps...'

For a long time Clara, who had been taking note of Robert's aesthetic development, had been urging him to tackle the larger forms. He himself hesitated before the complex world of the orchestra, although he burned to discover an ever-richer means of expression for his genius. 'I am tempted to smash my piano as it is

124

Clara (unknown painter)

becoming too narrow to contain my ideas. I really have very little practical experience of writing for the orchestra, but I don't despair of acquiring it...'

His first attempt dated as far back as 1832, and using his keen critical sense, he had decided to disown the symphonic movement which had been played at Zwickau at the time. He waited nine years before he repeated the experiment. Unstable, contradictory and passionate as Schumann was, the strictness and assuredness of his creative evolution were all the more striking. It seems that he never took up new modes of expression until he felt that they had already reached a perfect maturity within him. He then gave himself up to them impetuously, and dedicated himself completely to the form imposed by the latest transformation of his sensibility and his genius. After having exhausted the resources of the piano and having brought the art of the *lied* to its apex, Schumann felt that he had been called by the romantic symphony to follow in the wake of Beethoven, Schubert and Mendelssohn.

'February 14th, 1841: The Symphony has given me many happy hours and is now almost finished. I often give thanks to the beneficent spirit for allowing me to bring a work of this importance to a successful issue, in so little time and with such facility. The sketch of the entire Symphony was completed in four days. Exhaustion followed after the many sleepless nights.'

The Leipzig Gewandhaus

It was the 'Spring' Symphony, produced at the same time as Robert and Clara were together at work on the composition of the cycle *Liebesfrühling* (Op. 37).

'Could you', Schumann wrote much later to Taubert, 'breathe into your orchestra a little of the longing for spring? I myself felt full of it when I wrote the Symphony in January 1841. I should like the first phrase for the trumpets to be like a reveille sounding on high...'

As soon as it was composed, the Symphony was entrusted to Mendelssohn who performed it with 'untold care and attention' at a Gewandhaus concert.

'March 31st, concert by the Schumann couple. A happy evening of which we will preserve an unforgettable memory. Clara performed like a great artist and with a feeling of being carried away which ravished everyone. This day will also count among the most important in my life. My wife has understood this and she has been almost happier at the success of my Symphony than at her own... I should still have many things to write about this evening but I feel myself drawn by the new Overture I am working on, and so, my dear wife, you must forgive the brevity of these few lines...'

'From April 11th – 25th: I have worked hard and well: I orchestrated the Overture in C major in four days and took only four more days to complete a draft of a *Scherzo* and *Finale* for orchestra.'

127

A week after the sketch for this work, his Op. 52, Schumann started working on *Phantasie* in A minor for piano and orchestra, for Clara. Conceived as complete in itself, the work was nevertheless rounded off in 1845, by the addition of an *Intermezzo* and a *Finale*, and became the Piano Concerto in A minor (Op. 54), one of Schumann's masterpieces. As a composition it was completely introspective, and as far removed from the dramatic quality of Beethoven's concertos as from the pure and mannered virtuosity of the period. The Op. 54 was, in Schumann's own words, 'something in between a concerto, a symphony and a grand sonata.' The piano did not oppose the body of the orchestra but integrated itself with it. It carried on a conversation with each instrumental group, and the orchestration, which had the transparency of chamber music, was innocent of any desire to dominate on the part of the soloist.

The first movement (the original *Phantasie*) was in cyclic form. It was an *Allegro affettuoso* dominated by one theme, one of Schumann's most beautiful, which was stated by the piano after a few brilliant introductory bars.

A totality of concentrated and directed lines of force, the principal theme constituted in itself a complete musical microcosm. It rose to its culmination point when it brushed against the key of D minor, then it slowly resolved in a dying fall which completed this perfect arc. Schumann then enriched this theme with two secondary subjects, and made it sparkle so as to give life to the entire movement. He continued by transforming its elements, modulating from A minor into A major in the middle of the development section (one of the concerto's finest moments), and finally, in a vast *cadenza*, free from traditional demonstrations of virtuosity, he

128

ranged the voices of his divided self, drawn up for their final struggle. It was on an irresistible whirlwind of sound, a rhythmical transformation of the theme, that this first movement ended.

The *Intermezzo* and the *Finale*, composed in 1845, were in perfect harmony with it. The *Intermezzo* was an intimate dialogue between piano and orchestra, written very delicately and with the balance between the strings and the wind instruments perfectly worked out. The cello solo which came in the middle of the movement accentuated its chamber-music quality. In the last bars the woodwind prepared for the theme of the *Finale*, which was joined to it without interruption. Its theme burst forth on the piano, casting rays of joy and light. It was derived from the main theme of the first movement. And so, after an interval of four years, Schumann succeeded in impressing unity on the whole work, and the *Finale* became the necessary crowning-piece of the concerto.

Liszt, who had already felt in 1839 that the piano would become too narrow for Schumann, wrote to him at the time: 'I think I have already expressed to you in one of my previous letters the desire I had to see you write some *ensemble* pieces, – Trios, Quintets, Septets. Will you forgive me for insisting again on this point? It seems to me that success, even commercial success, will not be denied them.'

It was only in 1842 that Schumann yielded to his friend's solicitations, and suddenly there was a terrific spate of production. 'June 2nd 1842: Attempts at a Quartet. June 4th: started the Quartet in A minor. June 6th: Finished the *Adagio* of the Quartet. June 7th: Worked on the Quartet. June 8th: My Quartet almost finished. June 10th: Applied myself again to my Quartet. June 11th: A good day, started a Second Quartet. June 14th: The *Quasi Variazioni* movement of my Quartet. June 17th: Worked at the Second Quartet. June 18th: The Second Quartet almost finished up to the *Variazioni*. June 21st: Worked solidly on the Quartet. July 5th: Finished my Second Quartet. July 8th: Began the Third Quartet. July 10th: Worked with application on the Third Quartet.'

As with the *lieder* in 1840, and the symphonic forms in the previous year, Schumann had no respite until he had, in a feverish fit of creation, exhausted the newly discovered musical *genre*.

The quartet's form and the unified sonorities of its instruments imposed a strict discipline on the polyphonic complexity and harmonic refinement which characterised Schumann's thought. The intimate and inward qualities which chamber music possessed

129

suited Schumann better than the big forms, and he fully mastered this field in which he expressed himself most happily.

One can find certain characteristics of the First Symphony in the three String Quartets (Op. 41) as well as in more than one of the later chamber works: the very short lyrical introduction which led up to the opening *Allegro*, and a desire for thematic unity which was fulfilled by relating the themes of one movement to those of another. It was with this kind of tender and pensive introduction, treated in an exceedingly polyphonic style that the First Quartet in A Minor opened, and also the Third in A major. The contrasted *tempi*, dynamics, rhythms and fugal entries of the four instruments, gave these quartets, despite certain noticeable influences, a specifically Schumannesque character. Among their finest pages were those devoted to the *Quasi Variazioni* of the Second Quartet of which this was the theme:

In the Piano Quartet in E flat major (Op. 47) composed between October 24th and the end of November 1842, the *Allegro* was again preceded by a short introduction written in an exquisitely delicate manner: in a distant and mysterious echo the piano answered the strings' exposition of the theme. The entire quartet then attacked the *Allegro* and remained suspended in the middle of it waiting for the slow, nostalgic and plaintive theme of the opening to return. A lyrical *Adagio* followed a rather linear *Scherzo* with a double *trio* section. A fast-moving *Finale* recalled, perhaps unconsciously, the conclusion of Mozart's A major Piano Concerto.

The Quintet for piano, two violins, viola and cello (Op. 44), dedicated to Clara, dated from the same period (September-November 1842). This became one of Schumann's best known chamber works and was also the one which was laid-out in the most classical manner. Liszt, an ardent innovator, judged it severely, finding 'that it had too much of Leipzig about it' – a Leipzig synonymous with academic neo-classicism. In saying this, he most unjustly failed to recognise the extraordinary character of the second movement, a funeral march whose obsessive theme recurred without respite like an '*idée fixe*'.

The opening *Allegro Brillante* was a perfect model of sonata form: two themes met each other there, the one in E flat major, full of dash and spirit, the other, in the relative key of C minor, was more lyrical and imbued with a restrained tenderness. In their long development the piano played a dominant role, and asserted itself by opposing the strings.

The second movement, *In Modo d'una Marcia*, was one of Schumann's masterpieces. Three thematic ideas were developed in it with a strictness which gave the movement a truly grave and profound character.

The funereal rhythms of the first theme (A),

were succeeded by the long lament of the second (B), a static and immaterial melody.

The panting breath of the first theme was heard once more, then a third and more rhythmical idea was introduced (C):

A
B
A
C
A
B
A

The harshness of the piano part gradually became allayed and its place was taken by the purest harmony. The first theme then reappeared, and with it the other panel of the triptych, in which the first was reflected as in a mirror.

Following a vigorous *Scherzo*, the *Finale* brought back, in Schumann's favourite manner, the work's opening theme in a powerful series of fugal entries.

After this abundance of instrumental music, Schumann, following his rhythm of alternation, kept silent. This apparent sterility prepared the stage for the new metamorphosis of his inspiration.

Illustration to Paradise and the Peri *(Jones and Waner)*

Desiring always to create something bigger, to animate an ever-richer body of sound, Schumann's dreams were now of opera. 'How I aspire to write an opera! I have hardly had time to compose, having had so much trouble with the "*Peri*". Nevertheless, my mind has been occupied with several operatic projets . . .'

Das Paradies und die Peri (Op. 50) was like the foreshadowing of this desire. The work which was inspired by Thomas Moore's poem *Lalla Rookh* was a secular oratorio which sang of the triumph of pure love, and Schumann had derived it 'from his very heart's-blood'. The composer's breath could not bring to life this ever-angelic theme whose monotony was unrelieved. When the '*Peri*' was given its mediocre performance in December 1843, Schumann felt that the point of the work had not been grasped except by a few, and that its romanticism and orientalism had not been entirely understood.

At the same time as being enormously prolific as a composer, Schumann continued editing the review right up to 1844. The breadth of his vision, and his generous actions on behalf of all experiments which demanded courage, had made him known and esteemed by the whole of musical Europe. Attracted by the intelligence and ardour of Schumann and Mendelssohn, all the musicians of value then made their way to Leipzig.

'Mendelssohn', wrote the violinist Joachim 'was the greatest conductor I have seen both for interpretation and technique. He exercised an indescribable and electrical influence on his colleagues. He had made the Gewandhaus Orchestra, which he conducted,

Musicians of the Leipzig orchestra

into one of the best in Germany, and turned the Leipzig audience into one of the most hard to please.'

Schumann felt a profound admiration and friendship for the man who was at that time considered as Beethoven's successor. 'He is the most eminent man... a diamond fallen from the sky, the most cultured artistic nature of the period.' But this enthusiasm was also tempered by an extreme clear-sightedness – as some of his articles bear out – and in spite of a modesty which we find amazing, Schumann showed a true appreciation of his own worth: 'I know exactly where I stand in relation to him as a musician. He could go on teaching me things for years, but he, in his turn, could learn something from me. If, like him, I had been dedicated to music from my infancy, I should have flown higher than he has done – I can feel it with the force of my imagination.'

Mendelssohn's friendship had a favourable influence on Schumann's life as it brought him the esteem and the confident collaboration which enabled his art to flourish. Even in his work, Schumann bore the imprint of his wonderful friend, as he happened to have been inspired by his style and by his way of shaping a phrase the roundness of which he so much admired. It is certain that Mendelssohn's example, as well as Liszt's frequent requests, induced Schumann to compose chamber music, and the String Quartets are dedicated to him. And the more or less conscious desire to measure his strength against that of his friend in all forms of composition was not foreign to the undertaking of the Symphonies. Mendelssohn, moreover, did not cease to encourage his imitator of genius. 'Mendelssohn told me just as he was saying good-bye that he had had no opportunity to express how much my music (the Quartets) pleased him. I was very happy to hear it, since his opinion is the one which counts most with me... I have spent some hours confiding in Mendelssohn. The honours which have been bestowed on him have only made him even more modest and accessible. Perhaps he also feels that he has reached the peak of his glory and that he will not be able to mount any higher... How I rejoice that I belong to the beautiful and flourishing period which is our own. On all sides people are agitating in favour of good music and the general public is showing an extraordinary sympathy for our efforts.'

Schumann was more aware than his friend of the innovating currents of their time. And so he admired Berlioz, even though Mendelssohn found his orchestration 'so dirty that he had to wash his hand after turning over the pages of his scores.' Berlioz's journey to Leipzig in February 1843 was the occasion for an enthusiastic

GRAND OPÉRA.

GRANDE REPRÉSENTATION EXTRAORDINAIRE
DE
MALVENUTO CELLINI.
AVEC
PASQUINADES LITTÉRAIRES ET ARLEQUINADES
MUSICALES
A LA FIN DE LA PARADE UNE GRANDE STATUE SERA
COULÉE...... L'AUTEUR AUSSI.

meeting for Robert who had introduced the French composer's music to Germany. The judgment which he passed on him was full of sympathy as well as penetration: 'He conducted admirably. There is much in his music that is insufferable, but also a lot that is extremely intelligent and even full of genius. Sometimes he produces the effect on me of the helpless King Lear in person... I have taken a great liking to him...'

Even more cordial were Liszt's visits. Famous throughout the length and breadth of Europe, he generously devoted himself to

135

Liszt conducting

working on his friend's behalf, and often played the works of Schumann, who spoke of him with esteem in the review. His tumultuous arrivals were always noted with great joy in the conjugal diary. The champagne flowed in rivers, and his exceptional spirit and animation, personal as well as pianistic, took the whole of Leipzig by storm. In December 1841 he gave a concert together with Clara, whose sympathy and admiration were mingled with reserve: 'Most of all he gives me the impression of being a spoilt child. He is good, over-bearing, amiable, arrogant, noble and generous, often hard with others... Liszt can play as he likes, and the result is always full of interest even if one can often find faults of taste, particularly in his compositions which I cannot qualify in any other term than "awful"... I am very near to detesting him as a composer, but as virtuoso he has sent me into a transport of admiration.'

Robert's admiration was more candid, but the friendship between the two was still able to postpone the quarrel which broke out later at Dresden. Liszt had wanted to hear the Trios and the Quintet by Schumann; after making everyone wait for a long time out of sheer coquetry, and stung by the demon of contradiction, he passed a harsh judgment on the admirable Quintet, and then played as badly as possible. Finally he began to praise Meyerbeer, Robert's

136

'favourite enemy', in exorbitant terms, saying that beside him Mendelssohn did not exist. The quiet Schumann, who had by then reached the end of his tether, seized Liszt furiously by the shoulders and shouted at him: 'Who do you think you are to allow yourself to speak like that of a master like Mendelssohn!' then he withdrew to his room swearing that he had broken with Liszt for ever. The following year, however, the friends made up their quarrel: 'Let us forget that evening,' wrote Robert, 'a word is not an arrow. The important thing is always to go forward.'

At the beginning of 1844 Clara, who could not remain content with her successes in Leipzig, took Schumann through Berlin, Tilsit and Riga right the way to St. Petersburg and Moscow. For Clara it was a fruitful and glorious journey, for Robert a sorely trying one. Having quickly wearied of his early curiosities and enthusiasm, Schumann felt very low, both physically and morally. The Kremlin inspired him to write a few verses, – the only ones of his maturity – but in the midst of banquets and applause he found himself strangely deflated and out of his element. For a few months he went through an unproductive period which cast its gloom over him, and his contradictory moods manifested themselves in illnesses and nervous ailments which crowned his instability and melancholy. Nevertheless, as always in his moments of prostration and miserable helplessness, he devised grandiose projects for the future. As soon

as he had returned to Leipzig he applied himself to the second part of *Faust*, which he wanted to turn into a musical poem.

On it he exhausted his remaining powers and the results of overworking, – sleeplessness, attacks of weeping, and a hatred for music, – grew worse. He then gave up the editorship of the review which passed to Lorenz and then to Brendel. It was at that moment that Mendelssohn left Leipzig, taking with him much of the friendship and esteem which Schumann had found in the town of his adoption. He put himself forward as a candidate to succeed Mendelssohn as conductor of the Gewandhaus Orchestra, but the Saxon composer was passed over in favour of the Dane, Niels Gade, who was also hardly lacking in talent. From that time, Schumann, who had been bitterly disappointed, conceived a dislike for Leipzig. He was suffocating there and dreamed only of leaving the town which seemed to have repulsed him after ten years in which he had added so much to its musical renown. At the end of summer he and his family moved to Dresden where they were to stay for several years.

Manuscript of a poem by Schumann

The Dresden Theatre in 1841 (water-colour by Bäsler)

I am not working in vain

Dresden, the Royal capital of Saxony, was then the perfect picture of a musical desert. In its sumptuous rococo décor, it lived a sluggish life turned towards the past. Painting was traditionally encouraged there, display-painting, also opera. But twenty years earlier Weber himself had not been able to convert the public to German opera and great music. There was no orchestra, not even a good chamber ensemble, and Beethoven was not played there because he was not a draw. 'A famous periwig is still hanging on their back', Schumann wrote to Mendelssohn.

Why Schumann should have left Leipzig for such an atmosphere is baffling. Even more paradoxical was the presence of Wagner, the herald of the future, as '*Hofkapellmeister*' to the outdated Court. Would the two musical exiles at least bring each other help and consolation? It would have needed more than the forced esteem which never yet has crowned a feeling of real sympathy. Schumann judged Wagner as a 'clever fellow, but full of mad ideas', insufferably garrulous and provocative. The anarchism of this friend of Bakunin's shocked a man 'who by temperament disapproved of every form of disorder'. As for Wagner, he denigrated Mendelssohn and claimed with fanatical intransigence to have converted Schumann to his conception of the German opera. To the introspective romanticism of the one was opposed, without the possibility of reconciliation, the conquering romantic-

141

Hans von Bülow (F. Preller)

Wagner (Braun)

ism of the other, and these two geniuses did not know how to pool their efforts so as to stir up at Dresden the life-giving breeze of a renaissance.

The friendships which, despite everything, attached Robert and Clara to Dresden were for the most part with the painters and sculptors grouped around Hiller. Artists who were passing through provided them with the intelligent contacts they lacked in their isolation. The people who visited them included the pianist Hans von Bülow, Niels Gade, the new director of the Gewandhaus, Jenny Lind and Wilhelmine Schröder-Devrient, both incomparable singers and devoted friends who dedicated their fame to the master's *lieder*. And, of course, there was also Liszt.

Schumann had arrived at Dresden in a state of complete nervous and moral confusion. The impression of solitude and of having been uprooted, which the town fostered in him, served to slow down the already sluggish flow of his vitality, and completely dispersed his remaining liveliness. Working without inspiration, and incapable of tearing himself away from composition, Schumann exhausted himself in numerous vain attempts: 'A painful day – my condition worse... feeling miserable and melancholy... violent attack of nerves... another awful depression...' And it was only several months later

Manuscript of the Studien für den Pedal-Flügel

that Schumann emerged from this grey and unproductive state. In the spring of 1845 a 'cure by counterpoint' inspired him to compose the *Studien für den Pedal-Flugel*, then the *Six Fugues on the name of 'Bach'* and *Four Fugues* for piano, timid attempts which represented the recovery of a feeling of the creative urge, disciplined by a strict form which could sustain him. In 1845 there also appeared the last two movements of the magnificent Piano Concerto, started in 1841 under the title of *Phantasie*, and dedicated to Hiller. His spirit ravaged once more, Schumann tore out of himself, with a painful but beneficial effort, the Second Symphony in C major (Op. 61).

'I composed this Symphony,' he wrote to Otten, the conductor, 'in December 1845 when I had hardly got over my illness and I believe that a hearing of this work bears this out. It was only in the last movement that I began to feel myself again, and, in fact, once the work was finished, I began to get better. But it still reminds me of a dark period. Your sympathy has proved to me that in spite of that, such sorrowful times can awaken interest... and I was particularly happy to know that my mournful bassoon in the *Adagio* did not escape you, as I wrote that part with a special feeling of tenderness.'

As in some of Beethoven's most moving works, the spirit's resistance is evident in it, but the victory of the creative artist magnifies both the work and the person. The Symphony finished on a note of triumph.

Schumann's victory over his urge to withdraw from life was less speedy and less complete. He tried cure after cure in vain, his feeling of intolerance towards Dresden deepened and he joyfully greeted the idea of Clara's projected tour to Vienna. Besides, it was rather more than a tour which he had in mind: Clara would revive the memories of her triumphs, but Schumann would establish his work with the public and perhaps, if they combined their successes, they would be able to move to Vienna and find there the atmosphere which would be propitious to their aspirations. What glamour these charming and ungrateful towns must possess that they are for ever implanting illusions which are doomed to disappointment! The light charms of Vienna had, moreover, a beneficial effect upon Schumann: his spirits improved and he began to compose again. Nevertheless, these few months, from November 1846 to the end of March 1847, were called to an early account not even by disappointment, which had been the case during his first stay, but by actual impediments.

At first their reception seemed encouraging: Clara was treated with distinction by the Court and the new arrivals were surrounded with well-wishers such as the poets Grillparzer and Eichendorff, who exerted every effort on their behalf. Nevertheless Clara was disappointed by the reaction to her first concert, which did not evoke the same wonderful enthusiasm as her earlier performances. Her art had become more austere, she no longer had the easy charm of a child prodigy, and Wieck, that experienced impressario, was there no more. At the second concert, the Piano Quintet and the Variations for Two Pianos by Schumann attracted only a small audience; the third concert, which included the First Symphony and the Piano Concerto, was a complete fiasco, as far as the appreciation of Schumann's music was concerned. The Viennese remained inaccessible to all art that seemed introspective, especially that of the Saxon composer, which was over-modern and made no concessions or compromises. Only Jenny Lind, 'the Swedish nightingale', managed to save the evening, and she succeeded in disarming the hostile indifference of the public with her singing of the *lieder*. Clara's bitter regret was that she had been unable to do something which could succeed like 'a song from Jenny Lind'.

Prague, which had applauded Mozart and Beethoven at a time when Vienna booed them, paid the couple a consoling tribute of admiration. But all hope had vanished of their becoming established in Vienna. Robert could not make up his mind whether or not to return to Dresden, and it was then that he decided to snatch success at Berlin where *Das Paradies und die Peri* would serve as his credentials. But the work was indifferently performed by amateurs who

144

had had insufficient preparation, and the coldness on the part of the public and the critics was not dispersed by the two concerts which followed. Berlin, which had formerly been one of the centres of the boldest forms of romanticism, was now no better than Vienna at providing a fashionable refuge for a musician of Schumann's calibre.

And so he had to return to Dresden to live in a thankless atmosphere without resources other than those which he could find within himself. The four children born at Dresden, he already had two, brought Schumann untold happiness. 'Children are a blessing,' he said, 'and one can't have too many of them', Clara sometimes felt weighed down by so large a family, and by responsibilities which she could foresee more clearly than Robert, and was aware of the ever-increasing

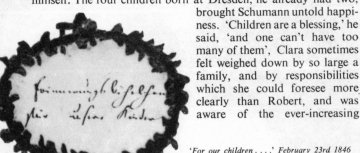

'For our children . . . .' February 23rd 1846

hindrances to her career. But Schumann, in spite of all the admiration he felt for the artist, thought that 'Clara herself believes that her principal mission in life is to be a mother and I think she is happy in a situation in which nothing else can be changed.' Schumann withdrew all the more readily into this quiet life – a walk at 11 o'clock with Clara, lunch with the children, an hour at the café before dinner – as his sufferings and his nervous afflictions, such as his phobias, hallucinations and disorders in his hearing, gave him no respite. For some years past, he had felt lazy about communicating with the outside world: 'I have difficulty in expressing myself in words or on paper, and a quarter of an hour at the piano enables me to say much more than if I had covered reams of paper with writing.'

In music, Schumann was always searching for a richer language, and his 'prayer from morning to evening was called German Opera', a supreme alliance of all the arts and an expression *par excellence* of the romantic soul. At twenty, he had already dreamed of bringing *Hamlet* to the operatic stage, and later *Doge und Dogaressa* by Hoffmann. The variety of subjects which had tempted him was incredible. Byron was on the list beside Goethe, Calderon and Thomas Moore. He considered the *Odyssey*, Racine's *Bajazet*, and *Sakuntala*, and even, it appears, the letters of Cicero! It was the

Performance of Genoveva, *at Leipzig*

medieval and romantic subject of Hebbel's *Genoveva* which he finally chose, and without waiting for the libretto, he composed the Overture in a few days in April 1846.

He wanted to make an anti-Meyerbeer protest out of his opera, and, following in Beethoven's and Weber's footsteps, to evoke a specifically national style to rival that of the Italian and the French opera. Schumann, who had already brought the tribute of his essentially German genius to romantic music, believed that he, rather than Wagner, who was still dependent upon foreign influences, had been called to fulfil the vow made by an entire generation. We know what was to be the outcome of this muted rivalry between the two composers.

The misfortunes of the virtuous Genevieve of Brabant, unjustly suspected of faithlessness, had been sung by Tieck in the idyllic tones of a fairy-tale, and by Hebbel in somewhat harsher accents. Incapable of choosing between these versions, Schumann entrusted his friend Reinick with the task of preparing a libretto in which the differing views of both poets would be reconciled. Reinick's oversentimental adaptation did not satisfy him either and he wrote the words of the third act himself. For such a pieced-together text, the score was also lacking in cohesion: the interest was slack and the

Performance of Le Prophète *at Leipzig*

unfolding of the drama artificial and clumsy. The slender plot languished under the weight of the long musical commentaries with which the composer had hoped to enrich it. Only a few passages stand out in this disappointing work, together with the Overture, in which its essential themes are mingled in music of a rich symphonic complexity.

Finished in August 1848, *Genoveva* was to have been immediately performed in Leipzig. Instead it had to wait two years as it was replaced at the last moment by Meyerbeer's *Le Prophète*, whose appearance Schumann had already noted in the review, by drawing the cross on a tombstone. The work only enjoyed a '*succès d'estime*' and Schumann was the only one to perceive the resonance of the wealth of inner feelings it contained. His later attempts at an opera were no happier, and he never seemed to progress further than the composition of Overtures. Those which he composed to the *Braut von Messina, Julius Caesar* and *Hermann und Dorothea* were symphonic works of great beauty, but Schumann never realised his dream of German opera.

Freed from the dangerous requirements of theatrical form, Schumann found a more peaceful and spontaneous means of expression in 'dramatic scenes' which linked the orchestra with the voice and chorus. At the same moment as he finished *Genoveva*, he began working on *Manfred*. Schumann had the feeling that Byron's poem, which although in dialogue was not destined for the stage, contained the form best suited to his purpose. And his hero, of all romantic heroes, was the one who in those years of inward struggle must have appealed to Schumann as the most faithful personification of his romanticism, drawn even closer to the edge of the mysterious abyss.

Manfred had loved his sister, and after her death had sought by magic means to forget her, while at the same time wishing to evoke her spirit. Being unable to appease his torment, he attempted to die and Astarte appeared before him to prophesy his end. He died surrounded by the genies he had conjured up, defying them and refusing

'Manfred' (engraving by Tony Johannot)

Ouverture.
Rasch. ♩ = 152.
Langsam ♩ = 63.
Flöten
Hoboen.
Clarinetten in B.
Fagotte.
2 Ventilhörner in Es
2 Waldhörner in Es.
Ventil=
3 Trompeten in Es.
Pauken in Es. B.
3 Posaunen.
Violine 1.
Violine 2.
Viola.
Violoncell.
Contrabass.
Solo
Langsam.
Rasch.

the help of a holy man. But in Schumann's version he finally found peace, while the striking of bells accompanied a Requiem.

Manfred marked a new attempt at combining the elements of poetry and music. As in *Schön' Hedwig* and the *Ballade vom Heide Knaben*, ballads taken from Hebbel and intended for declamation with piano accompaniment, Schumann elaborated his work round a spoken text. But the poem and the music, each as powerful and suggestive as the other, did not succeed in becoming unified, as the *lied* had done, into a new means of expression. Instead they remained strangers and weakened rather than illuminated each other. It was in the sung episodes of the work, or in the purely orchestral fragments, that Schumann's romantic genius burst out with full force: in the appearance of the Spirit of the Alps, the composer achieved orchestration of a wonderfully airy and delicate quality; the calling-up of Astarte had a powerfully evocative intensity, and the Overture, all that is generally played of this work, was a masterpiece.

The strenuous labour which Schumann always devoted to those works which opened up new territory was often interrupted by physical disability or inconsolable griefs. Mendelssohn's death in 1847 reawakened the obsessions and gloomy fears of his friend. Schumann, silent and isolated, then sought to preserve his balance by immersing himself in work connected with the *Liedertafel*, a Choral Society, which had been handed over to him by Hiller. With this choir he rediscovered the life-giving contact of Bach, Palestrina, and Beethoven, while he himself composed several pieces for chorus. The piano also brought him some happy moments and he composed the wonderful *Album für die Jugend*, which, for many of us, recalls our childhood, as well as the *Waldszenen* ('Forest Scenes', Op. 82) which contained the *Vogel als Prophet*, a masterpiece, and the striking *Verrufene Stelle*, inspired by a macabre poem by Hebbel.

But Schumann also returned to composing chamber music, and the Trios, together with the Quintet, were among his most successful works in this field. Within a formal and instrumental mould which remained classical in form, and in which the piano played an essential role, Schumann gave free rein to his tortured imagination.

He had been the first of the German musicians to replace the traditional Italian terminology, such as *Adagio*, *Allegro*, etc., with indications in German that were essentially psychological. The demands of a novel sensibility extended not only to the works themselves, but also to their interpretation, for the live indications in the nation's language established the work's climate for the executant in the most suggestive manner. As early as the *Phantasie* (Op. 17), for example, the first movement bore the direction: '*Durchaus Fantastisch und leidenschaftlich vorzutragen*' ('to be interpreted in a fantastic and passionate manner'). Re-established in the Quartet, in the Quintet and in the Symphonies, the directions were again given in German in the Trios. The first movement in the D minor Trio (Op. 63) bore the direction 'with energy and passion' and opened with a theme which recalled the Schumann of the *Kreisleriana* and the Piano Sonata in G minor – a Schumann set free and brimming over with lyricism and passion.

An essentially Schumannesque rhythmic *motif*

faced this melodic theme and assured the dynamic quality of its development. A peaceful section followed and, in the upper register, calm chords sustained a *cantilena* on the violin and cello derived from the first theme which, at the conclusion, re-assumed its original form.

Two rhythmic elements were placed in opposition in the second movement ('lively, but not too fast'), the one in equal quavers, the other, as in the first movement, in dotted ones. In the middle section of this movement a chromatic subject was heard treated as a canon by the three instruments. The former rhythmic fragment penetrated surreptitiously into this texture of fluid polyphony, and announced a reprise.

The *Adagio* ('slow, with a profoundly inward feeling') was full of anguish, and gasping as though it had reached its last breath. It was based upon a fundamental contradiction of rhythm and metre which was realised in the form of constant syncopations. The strings kept on transgressing the bar-lines with the object of abolishing them. The piano drew attention to them discreetly while recalling the presence of the strong beats, thus accentuating the tension of the conflict.

The *Finale* ('fiery') exploded into a theme full of joy and violent passion. In its middle section, as in the work's first movement, there was a sudden calm: above the delicate pulsations of the piano, the violin played a pure and almost transparent melody, like a distant call, of a profoundly romantic character.

The first theme returned and the accelerated *tempo* ('faster and faster') brought the work to a glittering conclusion.

To the Second Trio (Op. 80), a less colourful work, and the *Fantasiestücke* (Op. 88) in the form of a suite for piano, violin and cello whose sketches went back to 1842, was added three years later the Third Trio in G minor (Op. 110), composed at Düsseldorf. The tormented imagination and passionate atmosphere of the Op. 63 were to be found in it. The work was extremely full of movement, the melodic intervals were disjointed, and generally fragmentary, and the contrasts were very violent, particularly in the last movement. In the *Scherzo* the theme was heard of the Fourth Symphony, whose definitive version Schumann drafted in the same year, and by which he was obsessed.

The period was hardly propitious for meditation, and Schumann was to endure further self-laceration on account of his revolutionary sentiments. Europe was in revolt, and in May 1849 troubles broke out in Dresden. While Wagner ran to the barricades and burned with the exalted ardour of the revolution at Bakunin's side, Schumann left the town together with his family. In his rural refuge at Kreischa, although violence horrified him as much when used by the rebels as against them, he experienced the inner vibrations of a new democratic conviction. This inspired the 'Four Marches for the year 1849' (Op. 76)... 'republican marches born in a

veritable fever of enthusiasm', and the 'Revolutionary Part Songs' after Freiligrath, which, judged as subversive, were only published in 1914. 'To sing the joys and sorrows which move our time – this gift, I feel, has been granted to me in preference to many other men.'

Schumann was mistaken in this, and once this homage had been paid to the liberal aspirations of the period, he quickly turned away from the world's convulsions. His religious feelings, which had been fairly hazy up to that time, became articulate and started to become embodied in works which, if they were not among his best, proceeded from the depths of his heart: the Motet: *Verzweifle nicht im Schmerzenstal* ('Do not despair') with words by Rückert (Op. 93) which dated from the same May, was the first of them.

The old influence of Goethe, which had long been masked by a more instinctive connection with Jean-Paul, imposed itself on the mature Schumann because of its less subjective and better controlled complexity. At a time when Rückert, Geibel, and Byron had stirred in him a magnificent renaissance of the *lied*, his preference went to the cycle taken from *Wilhelm Meister* (Op. 98a) where Mignon and the harp-player expired in a melancholy akin to his own, and which crowned the *Requiem für Mignon* (Op. 98b) for soloists, chorus and orchestra, with a grandiose and all-pervasive pathos.

'What do I not owe to Goethe', wrote Schumann. It seemed as if the year 1849, 'the most fruitful year of his life', had taken this as its keynote, and that the especially picturesque romanticism of *Genoveva* and the accursed romanticism of *Manfred* were followed by a deeper and more serene form of romanticism, which derived from the influence of the follower of Apollo at Weimar.

Faust, the most important of his dramatic works, had obsessed Schumann for nearly ten years. In Goethe's dramatic masterpiece – rather than in his poems – he found a mystical thought and poetry for which he felt great sympathy, as well as echoes which were predestined to become embodied in his music. In *Faust*, particularly in the last section, he rediscovered that full alliance between words and sounds achieved in the *lieder* inspired by Eichendorff and Heine.

The thirteen scenes of the work, grouped into three parts, preceded by an Overture, had no musical or dramatic unity; the work did not constitute an indissoluble whole. Stretched over nine years, the composition of *Faust* reflected the fluctuations of Schumann's genius at the mercy of his inspiration, his exhaustion and his psychological cures. It was on his return from Russia

155

in 1844 that the composer undertook this work, so long desired, and immediately started on the last section of the second part of *Faust*, the one most charged with meaning. A long period of sterility interrupted his enthusiasm, but the obsessional nature of the work haunted him constantly. In 1847 and 1848 he completed this last section, then, in the following year, he set to work on the first and second.

Of the first three scenes, the third is the best developed: Gretchen's dialogue in the cathedral with the evil spirit, punctuated by a pitiless 'Dies irae'. The chorus's chords sustained by the brass, advanced in gigantic clusters of sound, crushing and prophetic. The effect was hallucinatory and it reached its climax in the *Judex ergo* which followed the lament of the woman who had sinned, in the mocking laughter of Mephistopheles.

'Ariel and the Sun' introduced us to the rather more mystical atmosphere of the second part of *Faust*, and Schumann followed Goethe's instruction, 'Ariel – song accompanied by aeolian harps,' and depicted this first scene with violins and harps. It was one of his most beautiful pages, the orchestration fluid to the point of being impalpable.

Starting with the midnight scene in which the 'four grey women' appeared – Misery, Debt, Care and Need – Schumann followed the order of the last scenes in the second part of *Faust*. In Faust's death scene fatality of time also spoke: 'Remain, you are so fair!'

Ver_wei _ le doch, du bist so schön!...

but the supplication was in vain, and the moment passed. At the very instant that Faust believed he saw the accomplishment of his dream, the lemurs, moving to an inexorable rhythm, hollowed out his tomb. They caught hold of him and a funeral march was heard, and then faded slowly in the distance.

The visions which were later to obsess Schumann more and more – he saw himself later on torn apart by the lemurs and carried off by angels – found here, strangely foreshadowed in the haunted poetry of Goethe, a transposition into music which transcended the problems of pure aesthetics. In this third part of the work

Goethe's text itself became music: it was there that Schumann's genius was most perfectly realised. Of all the musicians who wanted to write their own *Faust* (Liszt with his '*Faust* Symphonie', Berlioz, etc.) he was the only one to get close to the immanent truth of this work which has made so deep an impression on the whole of our western civilisation.

In the form in which it was presented in the summer of 1849, *Faust* was given simultaneously at the ceremonies marking the centenary of Goethe's birth, at Dresden, Leipzig and, most gratifying of all, at Weimar. 'This grand and beautiful work', Liszt wrote from Weimar to his friend, 'had made a most grand and beautiful impression.'

'I have never been more active or happy in my art,' Schumann wrote at the time. 'The tokens of sympathy, which reach me from far and near give me the feeling that I am not working completely in vain. And so we go on spinning and spinning our web and finally spin ourselves into it.' This productive year also witnessed the blossoming of numerous works for chorus, wind-instruments (the *Adagio und Allegro* for horn and piano, Op. 70, the *Fantasie-stücke* for clarinet and piano, Op. 73, and the *Concertstück* for four horns and orchestra, Op. 36). The year 1850 opened on a note of great hope – that of finally leaving Dresden. Hiller had given up the conductorship of the Düsseldorf Orchestra and had proposed that Schumann become his successor. The Rhinelanders were enamoured of good music and open to modern works. After much hesitation Schumann and Clara made their decision: 'We shall not remain at Dresden for anything in the world,' Clara wrote in the diary, 'we are terribly bored... there is not a musician in sight.'

In the autumn the new *Musikdirektor* arrived at Düsseldorf. A warm welcome awaited him and the town paid the composer its admiring homage. The free and benevolent atmosphere of the Rhineland gave Robert and Clara the promise of happy years ahead, and it was with a feeling of joy that Schumann got ready to mount the conductor's rostrum. Some fears, due to his lack of experience, were quickly disposed of. The orchestra was excellent, also the choir. Schumann did not doubt that he had at last found the position and the musical atmosphere which he had so long hoped for.

This feeling of serenity was propitious to his work: starting in October he composed the Cello Concerto (Op. 129) and in November and December, always with same immense speed, the 'Rhenish'

Symphony (Op. 97). Schumann wanted to subtitle it 'Accompaniment to a Solemn Ceremony' as it had been composed while the impression was still fresh in his mind of the pomp which had attended the enthronement, at Cologne, of the new Archbishop. It also contained a reference to the deep attraction which Schumann had felt since his youth for the '*Vater Rhein*', the protective divinity of Germany. His home was near the river and he was often lost in the contemplation of its waters. The following year Schumann,

'Evening on the Rhine' (C. Böttcher)

taking up the sketch which had already been performed in 1841, composed his last Symphony.

Schumann's four Symphonies, large and complex works, require an intensive analysis, going beyond the necessarily limited scope of this study. Rather than describe their movements, their developments and their themes with haste and imprecision, it would seem preferable to attempt a brief synthesis of the musical problems they pose.

More than any other works by Schumann, the four Symphonies revealed the struggle of a distracted and profoundly romantic imagination, and a spirit that sought to master it without changing its fundamental character. Romanticism, the immediate and instinctive expression of the ego, ere tended to exceed itself in the will to dominate its material, in a 'classical' conception not of style (as in the case of Brahms), but of artistic creation itself.

Under the pressure of an exceptional force, of romantic inspiration which embodied the smallest inflexions of the sensibility in figures of sound, there burst forth in Schumann's symphonic texture constantly new themes and special structures – such as the lyrical introduction which nearly always preceded the *Allegro*, or the reminiscences of earlier works – with the almost textual *motif* from the *Kreisleriana* (the eighth piece) in the *Finale* of the First Symphony, or one of the *Novelletten* which was quoted in the 'Rhenish'. The symphonic dimension in time and space (fulness of length, thickness of orchestral texture) still further accentuated, for an imagination which tended to disperse itself in richness, the perils of a collapse of unity. Schumann was not conscious of this menace in *Das Paradies und die Peri*, *Manfred*, or *Die Rose Pilgerfahrt*. He had relied on the factor which made for apparent unity, the poetic text, which nevertheless failed to give these works a truly internal cohesion. It was also in the tight and concise form of the Overture (*Manfred*, *Das Paradies und die Peri*) and in certain scenes from *Faust*, that Schumann's genius displayed itself to the best advantage. But it was in the Symphonies that the composer concentrated his astonishing effort to impose unity – a new kind of unity, for it was no longer possible for Schumann to return to the absolutely reliable traditional schemes, after their overthrow by the Ninth Symphony of Beethoven, or to repudiate his romanticism.

His imperious search for unity began as early as the First Symphony (Op. 38). The first theme of the introduction (inspired by a verse of Böttiger's *Im Tale blüht der Frühling auf*) generated the theme of the *Allegro* and reappeared in the *Finale*.

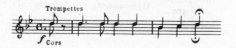

On the other hand, every solution of the problem of continuity between the second and third movements was suppressed. In the Second symphony in C major (Op. 61), the *Sostenuto* introduction foreshadowed the themes of the opening *Allegro* and those of the *Finale*, in which elements taken from the *Adagio* were also to be found. An unusual persistence throughout the work of the chord of the tonic (C major) towards which the *Adagio*, itself in a minor key, also led, revealed this preoccupation with cohesion extended even to the functions of key-relationships.

But in the Symphony in D minor (Op. 120), the first version of which was composed in 1841, and the second, after long maturing, ten years later, this search for unity, and therefore for a form that was novel, was still more striking. The original title of '*Symphonistische Fantasie*', demonstrated Schumann's desire to get away from the traditional symphonic restrictions. The movements of the work were linked without interruption, and the form was cyclic.

A main theme organised and welded together the outer movements. (This problem preoccupied Schumann for a long time: it was to be found again jotted down in a notebook filled-up during a lonely journey back from Hamburg where Schumann had left Clara.) In the first and last movements, the longest ones and the pillars of the Symphony, the theme appeared at the beginning in its original form, then in a shortened figure which was enriched by a new rhythm in the *Finale*. The other thematic elements followed the same principle of complex inter-relationship. The theme of the introduction, as important as the precedent, entirely determined the *Romanze* – underlying in the first fragment, and plainly visible in its middle section, just as the whole *Scherzo* – by an inversion of the theme of the opening, and then in the *trio* by means of a subtle chromatic variant...

```
                              ┌───┬───┬───┐
              ┌──────┘   ┌──┘     ↓       ↓
              ↓          ↓  A B A     A B A
I.   Introduction    II. Romance  III. Scherzo  IV. Finale
        Allegro
              ↑                            ↑
              └────────────────────────────┘
```

By creating an organic dependence between the episodes at the heart of a form whose traditional unity had been shaken by the demands of romantic sensibility and expression, Schumann gave us his personal conception of the symphony. Between Beethoven, who had disposed of all the restrictions, and Brahms, who had re-established them while bringing them into accord with his idea of a controlled romanticism, the Symphonies of Schumann,

The old bridge on the Rhine at Düsseldorf

the Fourth in particular, marked a vital date in the history of this musical form.

The judgment of our time is not unanimous: an over-traditional and sometimes heavy orchestration occasionally concealed the profound value of the Symphonies. In fact it was not Schumann, but Berlioz and Wagner who created the modern orchestra, and developed it, moreover, in opposite directions, not so much as a 'covering of sound', but as an essential element of the language joined to musical thought itself. The passionate search for a romantic form of the Symphony of which these four great works bear the mark, nevertheless conferred unusual greatness and intensity upon their lyrical aspiration.

The road is so long . . .

The years 1851–3 were the last years of Schumann's creative career. Enjoying a period of relative respite from his sufferings and his nervous ailments, he produced in haste and without relaxation. He returned to all the forms which had marked his evolution: to the piano with the *Drei Clavier Sonaten für die Jugend*, to the *lied* with the cycle by Elisabeth Kulmann, and to choral works. This was the period in which he composed the great Overtures, the last Piano Trio, the *Concertstück* for Piano and Orchestra, the Violin Sonatas, each of them written in a few days.

There was no shortage of new projects; the Oratorio for soloists, chorus and orchestra, a rich form in which Schumann believed he could give the best of himself, was always haunting him. He dreamed of writing a *Luther*. 'Listen well to all the folk-songs,' he wrote in his 'Advice to the Musician', 'they are an inexhaustible mine of the most beautiful melodies which will reveal the characteristics of different peoples to you'. He gathered some of these airs on the banks of the Rhine and one can find their echoes in the Third Symphony. His Oratorio he wanted to make into 'something popular, intelligible to all, townsfolk and peasants, corresponding to the character of the hero who was also a great man of the people . . .', a very striking prophecy of a path not yet explored by music for a large ensemble. This project came to nothing, but this new inspiration of Schumann's showed itself in *Der Rose Pilgerfahrt* (Op. 112), an

165

Oratorio related to the 'Peri' in form and expression, except that it was more German and rustic. *Der Rose Pilgerfahrt* suffered from the weakness of its libretto, and its music too was rather colourless. But Schumann's predilection for this form did not weary, and he employed it in *Des Sängers Fluch, Das Gluck von Edenhall*, taken from Uhland, and *Vom Pagen und der Königstochter* by Geibel.

Düsseldorf, placed at the Rehnisch crossroads, seemed to urge travel. Clara and Robert soon left for Southern Germany and continued into Switzerland, happy in their freedom. Some tours followed this pleasant escapade. At Brussels, at Antwerp and particularly in Holland they were given a triumphal reception: 'I have discovered to my great surprise', wrote Robert, 'that my music is more "at home" in Holland than in my Fatherland. Excellent performances of my Symphonies have been given everywhere, even the Second and the Third which are most difficult. And they have also performed *Der Rose Pilgerfahrt* at The Hague.' What happiness was Schumann's at feeling that he had at last been understood...

At Düsseldorf, the pleasure which Schumann had experienced at the thought of conducting an orchestra was soon to be poisoned. Having left it too late to come to the rostrum, and already too much withdrawn into himself and accustomed to following an inner music, he used to become absorbed in the works that were being

performed to the extent of forgetting all about his musicians. He would fall into a deep reverie, a state which was hardly compatible with the active and vigorously externalised concentration needed for conducting an orchestra. The orchestra and the chorus, thrown off their course by this lack of firm direction, soon slipped into a state of anarchy. At the start of the first season the newspapers were reticent, soon they became frankly hostile. The committee of the Musical Society felt it was being criticised, and rival organisations began to spring up. In 1852 an attack of cerebral anaemia kept Schumann from the rostrum for some time, and the public voted for Tausch to replace him. On his return from a cure at Scheveningen, Schumann, who had formerly been taciturn, now found speech increasingly difficult and embarrassing and was able to assert himself no longer. Nevertheless, he persisted, forced on by necessity, perhaps unaware of what hindered him: 'A sad exhaustion of my strength,' he noted, 'a period of painful suffering'. Whenever he conducted, Clara, who was in the hall for every performance, believed that she would see him faint.

His undeniable contribution to music was forgotten, and the opposition of the orchestra, the committee and the public became noticeable and soon came to a head. Schumann was brutally requested to resign. The Spring Festival of 1853 seemed, however, to quell this antagonism: as a composer, Schumann had a resounding success with the *Rheinweinlied*, composed especially for the occasion, and the Fourth Symphony. There were ovations and laurel-wreaths, but all the same his conducting of the *Messiah* was criticised. Finally he was only left with the conducting of his own works, and Tausch took his place. Schumann, sorrowful and humiliated, gave in and accepted the committee's conditions. 'I cannot say how defenceless I felt', wrote Clara who had received the delegation which brought this ultimatum from the committee, 'and how painful it was for me to be unable to spare Robert this bitterness... What would I have not given for us to be able to get away from here immediately, but when one has six children it is not so easy...'

Schumann dreamed once more of establishing himself at Vienna or Berlin, but his struggle was over and he felt it. More and more he withdrew from the world. His inspiration dried up and he turned towards the poets, and in the course of his readings collected for his 'Garden of Poets' all that had been written about music from Homer to Jean-Paul. Nevertheless, before he made his final farewell, Schumann received an assurance that his art would be understood and perpetuated.

167

In May 1853, Clara and Robert heard the violinist Joachim perform the Beethoven Concerto 'as I have never heard the violin played before,' said Clara; 'no virtuoso has ever made such an impression on me.' A great artist, a profoundly good man, and a true friend, Joachim brought to Schumann at the end of his life an admiration which he valued highly, and re-created an atmosphere of youthful and joyous musical ardour all around him. 'He is the only composer of our time', Joachim wrote of Schumann, 'through whom flows the same strong musical torrent as did through Beethoven and Schubert. He sings as his nature dictates, and he has the courage to say to all: "I cannot do otherwise". But only he can do that.' Schumann felt the breath of new life from this friendship: 'Morning and Evening with Joachim... Joachim wonderful... Joachim bewitches us all.'

'September 30th: Herr Brahms from Hamburg', the diary noted laconically. But Schumann was to announce this revelation in stronger terms in his last article, entitled 'New Paths'. 'We are now living in a great period for music. A young man has appeared who has moved us to our inmost depths with his wonderful music. I am convinced that he will create the greatest sensation in the musical world... I believe that Johannes is the true apostle who will also write revelations which hordes of Pharisees will be unable to decipher even after centuries.'

Surrounded by the faith of the generation which was to take up the torch, the master was able to withdraw from the thankless world which grudged him its appreciation, and find with Joachim and Brahms, with Clara beside him, the peaceful happiness which was in his real nature. In this year of 1853 his sufferings seemed fewer. He was 'so gay', said Clara, 'that I was myself enlivened by his contact'. His journal referred to: 'Beautiful hours... my 43rd birthday, much joy... warm, a wonderful starry sky... September 13th: a very joyful day, marvellous

168

weather, walk to Benrath, then a surprise at home... Clara's superb playing...'

'What finer wedding anniversary can there be', wrote Clara on September 12th 'than to be at the side of my dearly beloved husband... I cannot begin to express what I felt, but my heart overflowed with love and veneration for Robert and with gratitude to heaven for the infinite happiness it has granted me. What I am saying might seem presumptuous, but is it not true that I am the happiest woman on earth?'

As a last joy there was the journey in January 1854 to Hannover where Brahms and Joachim had prepared the triumph of a Schu-

Daguerreotype of 1850

mann Festival, a complete and happy triumph which made the composer forget what a bitter place Düsseldorf had become.

Inspiration returned once more and was responsible for the Overture which crowned the immense edifice of *Faust*, a *Concert Allegro mit Introduction* for piano and orchestra (Op. 134), a Violin Concerto, dedicated to Joachim, as well as a Violin Sonata written in collaboration with Brahms and Dietrich.

And then, finally, came Schumann's very last work, the *Gesänge der Frühe* ('Songs of the Dawn'). After the Symphonies, after *Faust*, it was to the piano that he turned for a last time, and it was to the piano that he entrusted this supreme and extraordinary message. 'These are some pieces', he wrote to his publisher, 'which translate an emotion at the approach of dawn. Rather than a picturesque description, they are the expression of a feeling.'

The *Gesänge der Frühe* were dedicated 'to the most noble poetess Bettina'. But Schumann, who was on the threshold of madness which he felt he had already crossed, gave them another title: '*An Diotima*' a secret dedication to the heroine of the mad Hölderlin.

The grave and calm chords formed by the contrapuntal treatment of a melody of great purity built up a legendary sound. This farewell to music made one think of Bach's last *chorale*, written on his deathbed, and Brahms's last *chorale* for organ. But beyond the inspiration and the styles, one felt the echo from one work to another of a sense of freedom, a complete serenity and an absolute purity of expression which were the supreme accomplishments of the genius who had reached his boundary.

The last word must be left to Schumann, and here is the first page of the *Gesänge der Frühe*, the final masterpiece of a romantic artist.

Were the 'Songs of the Dawn', his farewell to music, also a farewell to this world of revelation in which Schumann had known his first feelings of division, and from which he had derived his inspiration and nourished his life and genius? Such was not the romantic destiny. Like Hölderlin and Hoffmann he would exceed his impulse but he would not let it die.

The calm middle-class life he led was only a dyke to prevent the onrush of a world of which he would no longer have been the master. For a long time Schumann had been aware of the threat of madness, the trap for those who have gone too far. So as to be able to capture in his song the call of that hidden universe which the romantics believed to contain the source of their inspiration, he had banished it from his daily life. As a masterful Faust, he knew how to evoke it and conjure it up according to his desire. The wise rules of the life, and the meticulous order which he brought to his thought and his contacts with the outside world, were so many exorcisms.

But the moment came when the exhausted imagination no longer created inner harmonies, and the salutary order was nothing more than gloomy silence. It was too late to return among men, the road was already too long, and the now silent poet had been so bruised by the world that in desperation he wished to climb back again into the heights which his song had made him reach. Schumann then devoted himself to occultism. He used all his visionary faith for table-turning: 'the tables know all', he said. This was not the play of an imagination that was henceforward sterile. In his reading he sought the same mediation of an inspiration which would supplement his own. He bothered himself no longer collecting tame quotations for the 'Garden of Poets', it was to Jean-Paul, who had originally awakened his evocatory power, that he returned.

In February 1854 Schumann was afflicted by the troubles which had now become habitual – difficulties of speech and disorders to do with his hearing, and the way he constantly heard the note A. He became more and more obsessed by the fear of the attacks becoming prolonged and he was haunted by the idea of going mad. 'Music is dead, at least outwardly', he wrote to Joachim. Suddenly, on February 10th, it was resurrected in him.

The unbearable note of A came to life with an existence of its own, and was changed into a terrible music which pierced through him relentlessly. 'Robert suffers terribly', Clara wrote in her diary. 'All sounds are transformed for him into music, and he says that it is a magnificent music, with instruments which resound so splendidly that their like has never been heard before on earth.'

172

(Drawing by Louis Boulanger)

It seems as it Schumann entered this world of suffering and light by progressive stages. He collected its sorrows and its joys one by one. This music, which he was no longer able to master, was so desperately beautiful, and its abundance was so intoxicating after the silence of the last months. Schumann struggled modestly against this feeling of ecstasy, which he realised was part of a mortal illness, but also with courage, as he had always done. As a counter-measure to this obsessive music, he used work of the most reasonable and least imaginative kind – such as correcting his Cello Concerto. In this progress towards madness, Clara who had remained with her reason unimpaired, accompanied him at a distance with all the strength of her helpless love. All through the night of February 17th she heard him rambling in his speech as he lay with his eyes open. He heard angels flying all around him and in the morning their places were taken by devils, in the shapes of tigers and hyenas to the accompaniment of 'dreadful music'. These periods alternated with moments of sanity. 'Soon', said Clara 'he cried out with pain... I suffered with him the most cruel torments', soon, writing at the dictation of angels, 'his gaze assumed an expression of beatitude that I shall never forget, even though that supernatural beatitude was as heart-rending as when the evil spirits had made him suffer.'

On February 21st the crisis seemed to be past, the voices had become silent and Schumann wrote some letters and played a sonata. But he believed he was a criminal and sometimes he asked Clara to keep away from him as he was afraid he might do her some

harm. Then he suddenly became aware of his state: the fear of his entire life had been realised – he was mad. 'Suddenly at half past nine he jumped up from the sofa, asked for his outdoor clothes, saying that he wanted to go to an asylum, that he had lost control over himself and that he did not know what he might be capable of doing during the night. He carefully collected everything he wanted to take with him, his watch, money, music-paper, pens, cigars, all most methodically. When I said to him: "Robert, you don't want to leave your wife and children," he answered me: "It won't be for long, I'll soon come back, cured".'

His obsession of guilt developed. Pursued by it and not knowing how to escape it, he left home on the morning of February 27th and threw himself into the Rhine.

Act of insanity, or act of lucid despair? 'Calm, peaceful, grave, and proud as an old German God', just as he saw it in his youth, would the Rhine give him the peace which had fled from him? Schumann had no refuge from his tormented journey beyond reason, not even death. Some boatmen saved him and brought him home.

Henceforward, a shadow of his former self, Robert Schumann was treated like a madman. Clara, who was expecting her eighth child, was hurried away. They took him to the small asylum at Endenich, near Bonn, where he lived for more than two years. He himself desired this separation as he hoped to be cured, and feared that he might do some harm to his children as the result of a sudden fit.

He was not confined, and received visits from Brahms and Joachim. He had a piano, and he would go for walks. He also plotted imaginary journeys on an atlas.

'In Schumann's case,' wrote his doctor, Dr. Richarz, 'awareness was dulled and bruised, but not destroyed. His ego had not become a stranger to him, nor had it changed. The melancholy which brought him to this place did not leave until the day the thread of his life snapped.'

If he had any hope of being cured when he arrived at Endenich, it seems that he soon felt further and further away from everything he had left behind him.

'Oh! If only I could see you again and speak to you once more. But the road is so long! I should like to know so many things, how your life is, where you are living, and whether you play as magnificently now as you used to...

'Could you send me something interesting – some poems by Scherenberg, a few old volumes of my review and my "Advice to Musicians"? I am also short of music paper as I sometimes like to compose a little. My life is very simple...'

Soon he no longer wished to receive visits and he wrote

The asylum at Endenich

no more. On July 23rd 1856, Schumann, who had ceased to take nourishment, lay dying. When Clara, who had hurried to Endenich, was at last able to see him, 'he smiled at me,' she wrote, 'and with a great effort clasped me with one of his arms. And I would not give up that embrace for all the treasures on earth.'

He died on the afternoon of July 29th, after several hours of terrible suffering.

Was it not for him, who had reached the horizon of his nocturnal journey, that Hölderlin might have intended these verses:

> '... That someone might extend to me,
> Full of the gloomy light,
> The perfumed cup from which to take repose
> For in the shadows sleep will be so sweet.
> Of this once dispossessed, now he is vain
> Of being nothing more than mortal thoughts...'

Clara (unknown painter)

Vorbemerkung.

Wir geben hier einmal über Ein Werk zwey
Beurtheilungen; die erste von einem jungen Manne,
einem Zöglinge der neusten Zeit, der sich genannt
hat; die andere von einem angesehenen und wür-
digen Repräsentanten der ältern Schule, der sich
nicht genannt hat: allein, wir versichern und haben
es kaum nöthig, von einem durchaus tüchtigen, voll-
geübt und umsichtig kenntnissreichen.

Wir meinen, durch diese Zusammenstellung
nicht nur unsere Aufmerksamkeit auf den Verf. des
zu besprechenden Werkes auf hier ungewöhnliche
Weise an den Tag zu legen, sondern auch zu-
gleich, und ganz besonders, unseren geehrten Le-
sern zu mancherley eigenen und höchst nützlichen
Vergleichungen Veranlassung zu bieten, die mit
ihrem grossen Nutzen eine Unterhaltung gewähren,
die zu viel Anziehendes hat, als dass sie irgend
einem denkenden Musikfreunde anders als höchst
willkommen seyn könnte. Mit dem Werke in der
Hand wird es wohl am glücklichsten gelingen.

Die Redaction.

I. Von K. Schumann.

Ein Opus II.

— — — Eusebius trat neulich leise zur Thüre
herein. Du kennst das ironische Lächeln auf dem
blassen Gesichte, mit dem er zu spannen sucht.
Ich sass mit Florestan am Klavier. Florestan ist,
wie Du weisst, einer von den seltenen Musikmen-
schen, die alles Zukünftige, Neue, Ausserordent-
liche schon wie lange vorher geahnt haben; das
Seltsame ist ihnen im andern Augenblicke nicht
seltsam mehr; das Ungewöhnliche wird im Moment
ihr Eigenthum. Eusebius hingegen, so schwär-
merisch als gelassen, zieht Blüthe nach Blüthe aus;
er fasst schwerer, aber sicherer an, geniesst seltener,

aber langsamer und länger; dann ist auch sein Stu-
dium strenger und sein Vortrag im Klavier-
besonnener, aber auch zarter und mechanisch voll-
endeter, als der Florestans. — Mit den Worten
„Hut ab, ihr Herren, ein Genie," legte Eusebius
ein Musikstück auf, das wir leicht als einen
aus dem Haslinger'schen Odeon erkannten. Den
Titel durften wir weiter nicht sehen. Ich blätterte
gedankenlos im Buche; dies verhüllte Genies-
sen der Musik ohne Töne hat etwas Zauberisches.
Ueberdiess scheint mir, hat jeder Componist seine
eigenthümlichen Notengestaltungen für das Auge:
Beethoven sieht anders auf dem Papier, als Mozart,
wie Jean Paul'sche Prosa anders, als Göthe'sche.
Hier aber war mir's, als blickten mich lauter fremde
Augen, Blumenaugen, Basiliskenaugen, Pfauenaugen,
Mädchenaugen wundersam an: an manchen Stellen
ward es lichter — ich glaubte Mozart's „Là ci darem la mano" durch hundert Accorde geschlungen zu sehen, Leporello schien mich ordentlich wie anzuzwin-
keln und Don Juan flog in weissen Mantel vorüber. „Nun spiel's," meinte Florestan lachend und
Eusebius. „wir wollen Dir die Ohren und die
Augen zuhalten." Eusebius gewährte; in einer Fen-
sternische gedrückt hörten wir zu. Eusebius spielte
wie begeistert und führte unzählige Gestalten des
lebendigsten Lebens vorüber; es ist, als wenn der
frische Geist des Augenblicks die Finger über die
Mechanik hinaushebt. Freylich bestand Florestans
ganzer Beyfall, ein seliges Lächeln abgerechnet,
nichts als in den Worten: dass die Variationen
etwa von Beethoven oder Franz Schubert seyn
könnten, wären sie nämlich Klavier-Virtuosen ge-
wesen — wie er aber nach dem Titelblatte
weiter nichts las, als:

Là ci darem la mano, varié pour le Piano-
forte par Frédéric Chopin, Opus 2,
und wie wir beyde verwundert ausriefen: ein Opus
zwey und wie Eusebius hinzufügte: Wien,

49

Title-page of the Kreisleriana.

Frédéric Chopin

Eusebius appeared the other day, opening the door very quietly. You know the ironic smile on this pale face with which he seeks to arouse curiosity. I was sitting at the piano with Florestan. Florestan, is as you know, one of these rare musicians who can anticipate, far in advance, anything that the future may hold of the new and the extraordinary. But he had a surprise that day. 'Hats off, gentlemen, a genius', said Eusebius and he showed us a piece of music whose title we could not see.

I turned over the pages unconsciously, the veiled enjoyment of music one does not hear has something magical in it. And besides it seemed to me that every composer has in his notes entirely personal characteristics which speak to the eye; Beethoven looks very different from Mozart on paper, rather like the way Jean-Paul's prose differs from Goethe's.

But here it seemed to me as if eyes were watching me in a very strange manner; flower eyes, basilisk eyes, peacock's eyes, maiden's eyes, in many places it was brighter – I thought I saw Mozart's *La ci darem la mano* struck by a hundred chords. Leporello really appeared to me, winking, and Don Juan flew past me in his white mantle.

'Now play it', said Florestan. Eusebius consented; in the recess of a window we listened. Eusebius played as though inspired and made countless personages pass before us filled with the liveliest life; it seemed that the enthusiasm of the moment gave his fingers a facility beyond the usual measure of his powers.

179

Schumann's article on Chopin.
'*Hats off, gentlemen, a genius . . .*'
('Hut ab, ihr Herren, ein Genie')

Réminiscences: Chopin. Georges Sand. Belle
jeunesse. Parfums. Rayons de lune. Amour.

Drawing by Janko, 1873

Richard Wagner

Without doubt Wagner is a clever fellow, full of mad ideas and bold to
a degree, but he does not know how to write or think out four consecutive
bars which are beautiful or even correct. What they all lack is the knowledge of how to write a four-part chorale. This music is not a bit better
than Rienzi, in fact it is more pallid and forced.

Regarding *Tannhäuser*, I must take back what I said after reading the
score. On the stage the impression is quite different. I was moved by
numerous passages. *Tannhäuser* contains things that are profound,
original and a hundred times superior to his earlier operas. In short,
it may be destined for a great place in the history of the stage.

180

Extracts from Master Raro's, Florestan's and Eusebius's Journal of Poetry and Thought

It is foolish to say that we cannot understand the music of Beethoven's last period. Why? Is it so difficult harmonically? Is it so unusual from the point of view of construction? Is there too much contrast between the thoughts? It must be something like this, for in music, in general, even a madman cannot suppress harmonic laws. But he can always be more insipid.

The extraordinary in an artist (and it is to his advantage) is not to be always immediately appreciated.

The Leonora Overture

Beethoven must have wept when it was played for the first time in Vienna and almost wholly failed; Rossini, in the same situation, would have laughed all the more. Beethoven was induced to write a new one in E major, which might have been written by some other composer. Thou didst err; but thy tears were noble. (Eusebius)

The cultivated musician may study a Madonna by Raphael, the painter a symphony by Mozart, with equal advantage. Even more: in the sculptor the actor's art becomes fixed, the actor transforms the sculptor's work into living forms; the painter turns a poem into a painting, the musician sets a picture to music. (Eusebius)

Paganini is the turning point of virtuosity.

'Paganini, master-magician' (Lyser)

Rules of Conduct for the Musician

You must practice scales and other finger exercises conscientiously, but that is not enough. There are plenty of people who think they may achieve everything by devoting several hours a day to mechanical exercises. That is as reasonable as trying to recite the alphabet faster and faster every day.

The man who has not read the most notable books published recently counts as an illiterate. We ought to be as advanced when it comes to music.

Don't be afraid of the words 'theory', 'thorough-bass', 'counterpoint', etc. They will give you a friendly welcome, if you do the same for them.
Never strum. Always play carefully and never try a piece half through.

Try to play easy pieces gracefully and well; it is better than to play difficult ones badly.

It is not enough to be able to play your pieces with your fingers; you should be able to hum them without a piano. Sharpen your imagination so that you may be able to remember not only the melody of a piece, but also its proper harmonies.

You must acquire the power of being able to read every piece of music and understand it simply by reading it.

Always play as though a master were listening to you.

Never lose an opportunity of making music with others, in duos, trios, etc. These exercises will make your playing more fluent and spirited. Accompany singers often.

Work hard at the fugues of good masters; above all those of J. S. Bach. Let the 'Well-tempered Clavier' be your daily bread. You will then certainly become a good musician.

But what does it mean to be called a 'musician'? You are not one when, with eyes anxiously fixed on the music, you have trouble getting to the end of your piece; you are not one when you stop short and cannot carry on because someone has turned over two pages at once. But you are one when, in playing a new piece, you can foresee, near enough, what is going to follow, and when you play an old one, you know it by heart, – in short, when you have music not only in your fingers but also in your head and heart.

'Melody' is the amateur's war-cry, and certainly music without melody is not music. But understand well what they mean by that: for them it takes the place of anything that is easy to remember which has a pleasant rhythm. But it is, nevertheless, of a very different nature. And when you go through Bach, Mozart, Beethoven, they will appear to you in a thousand different forms; you will be, I hope, surfeited very soon with the monotony of what is called 'melody', and occurs principally in modern Italian operas, once you know these.

The laws of morality are also the laws of art.

Bibliography

ABERT, HERMANN: *Robert Schumann* (Berlin, 1903)

ABRAHAM, GERALD (Ed.): *Schumann, A Symposium* (London, 1952)

BÖTTICHER, WOLFGANG: *Robert Schumann: Einführung in Persönlichkeit und Werk* (Berlin, 1941)

CHISSELL, JOAN: *Schumann* (London, 1948)

ERLER, HERMANN: *Robert Schumann's Leben und Werke, aus seinen Briefen geschildert*, 2 vols (Leipzig, 1887)

HERBERT, MAY: *The Life of Robert Schumann told in his Letters* (London, 1890)

JANSEN, GUSTAV: *Die Davidsbündler: Aus Robert Schumanns Sturm und Drang Periode* (Leipzig, 1883)

LISZT, FRANZ: *Robert Schumann* (in *Gesammelte Werke*, Vol. IV, Leipzig, 1882)

LITZMANN, BERTHOLD: *Clara Schumann: ein Künstlerleben nach Tagebüchern und Briefen*. 3 vols. (Leipzig 1902-8) Abridged English translation by Grace E. Hadow. 2 vols. (London, 1913)

NIECKS, FREDERICK: *Robert Schumann: a supplementary and corrective biography* (London, 1925)

PITROU, ROBERT: *La vie intérieure de Robert Schumann* (Paris, 1925)

REISSMANN, AUGUST: *Robert Schumann, seine Leben und seine Werke* (Leipzig, 1879). English version, *The Life of Schumann* by A. L. Alger (London, 1886)

SCHAUFFLER, ROBERT H: Florestan: *The Life and Work of Robert Schumann* (New York, 1945)

SCHUMANN, CLARA: *Robert Schumanns Jugendbriefe* (Leipzig, 1885) English version (London, 1888)

SCHUMANN, EUGENIE: *Memoirs* (London, 1930) *Ein Lebensbild meines Vaters* (Leipzig, 1931)

SCHUMANN, ROBERT: *Gesammelte Schriften über Musik und Musiker*. 4 vols (Leipzig, 1854). English version, 2 vols. (London, 1877). New translation, selection in 1 vol, (London, 1947)

STORCK, KARL: *The Letters of Robert Schumann* (London, 1907)

WASIELEWSKI, W. J. VON: *Robert Schumann: Eine Biographie* (Dresden, 1858) English version (London, 1886). Greatly enlarged edition (Leipzig, 1906).

Chronology

Schumann	The Others
	Novalis dies.
	Hölderlin becomes insane.
	Berlioz born.
	Schiller dies.
	Beethoven's Fifth Symphony.
	Mendelssohn born.
June 8th: Robert Schumann born.	Chopin born.
	Liszt born; Kleist commits suicide.
	Wagner born; Verdi born; Battle of Leipzig.
	Congress of Vienna.
	Schubert composes *Gretchen am Spinnrade:* Goethe writes the *Westöstliche Diwan.*
Schumann hears Moscheles at Carlsbad.	Clara Wieck born.
	Weber's *Der Freischütz.*
	Death of E. T. A. Hoffmann.
	Beethoven's Ninth Symphony.
Earliest literary attempts.	Jean-Paul Richter dies.
Schumann's father dies.	Weber dies; Mendelssohn's Overture to *A Midsummer Night's Dream.*
Attempts at *lieder*-writing.	Beethoven dies.
Schumann finishes his secondary studies and leaves for Leipzig where he enters the university as a law student.	Schubert dies.
Journey to Italy; stay in Heidelberg.	Mendelssohn conducts the first performance of the *St. Matthew Passion* since the death of Bach.

	Schumann	The Works
—1830	Schumann hears Paganini; becomes aware of his musical vocation and returns to Leipzig as a pupil of Wieck.	'Abegg' Variations (Op. 1); *Papillons* (Op. 2); *Toccata* (Op. 7).
1832	Paralysis of his right hand.	Studies after Paganini's 'Capri (Op. 3).
1833	Violent attack of nervous depression; foundation of the *Davidsbündler*.	Impromptus on a theme by Cl Wieck (Op. 5); Second set Studies after Paganini's 'Capri (Op. 10).
1834	April 3rd: First number of the *Neue Zeitschrift für Musik*.	*Études Symphoniques* (Op. 13)
1835	Becomes engaged to Ernestine von Fricken; discovers he is in love with Clara Wieck.	*Carnaval* (Op. 9); First Piano Sor Sonata in F Sharp minor (Op.
1836	Schumann's mother dies; Clara and Robert are separated by Wieck.	*Phantasie* (Op. 17).
1837	Clara plays the *Études Symphoniques* at the Gewandhaus.	*Davidsbündlertänze* (Op. 6); *Fantasiestücke* (Op. 12).
—1838	Visits Vienna.	*Kinderscenen* (Op. 15); *Kreisleri* (Op. 16); *Novelletten* (Op. Second Piano Sonata in G m (Op. 22).
1839	Because of Wieck's refusal to consent to their marriage, Clara and Robert apply to the legal authorities for permission to marry.	*Blumenstücke* (Op. 19); *Humor* (Op. 20); *Nachtstücke* (Op. *Faschingsschwank aus Wien* (26).
—1840	September 12th: Schumann marries Clara.	138 *Lieder*.
1841	'Few events, much happiness'; The First Symphony is performed in March.	First Symphony in B flat (Op.
1842		Three String Quartets (Op. Piano Quintet in E flat m (Op. 44); Piano Quartet in E major (Op. 47).
1843		*Das Paradies und die Peri* (Op.
—1844	Visits Russia; settles in Dresden.	The last scene of *Faust*.
1845		Piano Concerto in A minor (54); begins Second Symphon C major (Op. 61) in Decem
1846	Tries to move to Vienna or Berlin.	
1847		Piano Trios in D minor and F m (Opp. 63, 80); starts work on Opera *Genoveva* (Op. 81).
1848		Finishes *Genoveva*; *Manfred* (115); cycle of song from *Will Meister* (Op. 98a); Scenes f *Faust*; pieces for horn, clari and oboe.

The Others

Schumann	The Works
— 1849 Schumann's 'fruitful year'. He flees from the revolution and takes refuge at Kreischa.	*Waldscenen* (Op. 82).
— 1850 Schumann accepts the post of *Musikdirector* at Düsseldorf.	Cello Concerto in A minor (O. 129).
1851	*Der Rose Pilgerfahrt* (Op. 112); t Grand Overtures; Third Piar in G minor Trio (Op. 110); Tw Violin Sonatas; Fourth Symph ny in D minor (Op. 121).
1852 First signs of discord between Schumann and the committee of the Musical Society. *Manfred* is performed at Weimar and the First Symphony at Düsseldorf.	*Requiem für Mignon* (Op. 98 Cantatas; *Bunte Blätter* (Op. 99
— 1853 Musical Festival at Düsseldorf. Schumann meets Joachim, then Brahms.	*Faust* Overture; Violin Concert *Gesänge der Frühe* (Op. 133).
1854 Hanover Festival; Becomes mentally deranged and attempts suicide. Schumann is taken to the asylum at Endenich.	
1856 July 28th: Schumann dies.	
1896 May 20th: Clara dies.	

A selected discography from Great Britain and America

CHAMBER MUSIC

Piano Quartet in E flat Major (Op. 47)
Piano Quintet in E flat Major (Op. 44)
Walter Bohle (piano) and the Barchet Quartet   Vox PL 8960 (G.B.)

Piano Quintet in E flat Major (Op. 44)
Curzon (piano) and the Budapest Quartet   Columbia 4ML-4426 (U.S.A.)

Piano Trio No. 1 in D minor (Op. 63)
Piano Trio No. 3 in G minor (Op. 110)
Trio di Bolzano   Vox PL 9920 (G.B. & U.S.A.)

String Quartet in A minor (Op. 41, No. 1)
String Quartet in A major (Op. 41, No. 3)
Curtis String Quartet   Nixa WLP 5166 (G.B.)
Westminster 5166 XWN-18495 (U.S.A.)

Sonata for Violin and Piano in A minor (Op. 105)
Wolfgang Schneiderhan (piano) and Carl Seeman (piano)
Deutsche-Grammophon ep. 130206 (G.B.)

CONCERTOS

Piano Concerto in A minor (Op. 54)
Dinu Lipatti and the Philharmonia Orchestra, conducted by Herbert von
Karajan   Columbia 33C 1001 (G.B.)   Columbia 4 ML 4525 (U.S.A.)
(Grieg: Piano Concerto)

Cello Concerto in A minor (Op. 129)
Pablo Casals and the Prades Festival Orchestra
Philips ABR 4035 (G.B.)   Columbia 5 ML 4926 (U.S.A.)

ORCHESTRAL MUSIC

Manfred Overture (Op. 115) (Smetana:Vltava)

The Vienna Philharmonic Orchestra conducted by Wilhelm Furtwängler
HMV BLP 1009 (G.B.)
NBC Symphony Orchestra conducted by Arturo Toscanini Victor LM 9022
(U.S.A.) (Beethoven: Overture: Schubert: Symphony 6)

Overture, Scherzo and Finale (Op. 52)
Symphony No. 2 in C major (Op. 61)

The Israel Philharmonic Orchestra, conducted by Paul Kletzki
Columbia 33CX 1449 G.B.) Angel D-35373 (U.S.A.)

Symphony No. 1 in B flat major (Op. 38)
Symphony No. 4 in D minor (Op. 120)

The London Symphony Orchestra, conducted by Josef Krips
Decca LXT 5347 (G.B.) London LL-1736 (U.S.A.)

Symphony No. 3 in E flat major (Op. 97)

The Berlin Philharmonic Orchestra, conducted by Ferdinand Leitner
Deutsche-Grammophon DG 16084 (G.B.)
Paris Conservatoire Orchestra, conducted by Carl Schuricht
London LL-1037 (U.S.A.) (Overture, Scherzo and Finale)

PIANO MUSIC

Carnaval (Op. 9)
Études Symphoniques (Op. 13)

Alfred Cortot HMV ALP 1142 (G.B.)

Carnaval (Op. 9)

Rachmaninoff Camden 396 (U.S.A.) (Chopin: Sonata B flat Minor,
Op. 35)

Davidsbündlertänze (Op. 6)
Sonata in F major (Op. 14)

Friedrich Wührer Vox PL 8860 (G.B. & U.S.A.)

Fantasiestücke (Op. 12)
Waldscenen (Op. 82)

Sviotislav Richter Deutsche-Grammophon DGM 18355 (G.B.)
Decca 9921 (U.S.A.)

Humoreske in B flat major (Op. 20)
Sonata No. 2 in G minor (Op. 22)

Jeorg Demus Nixa WLP 5264 (G.B.) Westminster WXN 18496 (U.S.A.)

Kreisleriana (Op. 16)
Études Symphoniques (Op. 13)

Wilhelm Kempff Deutsche-Grammophon DGG 19077 (G.B.)
Decca 9948 (U.S.A.)

Kinderscenen (Op. 16)

Walter Gieseking
(Debussy: Children's Corner Suite) Columbia 33C 1014 (G.B.)

Kinderscenen (Op. 16)

(Chopin: Mazurkas)
Horowitz   Victor LVT 1032 (U.S.A.)

Novelletten (Op. 21)

Jacqueline Blancard   Decca LXT 5120 (G.B.)

Phantasie in C major (Op. 17)

Andor Foldes   Deutsche-Grammophon DG 16076 (G.B.)   Clifford Curzon
London LL 1009 (U.S.A.) (Kinderscenen)

SONG CYCLES
Dichterliebe (Op. 48)

Aksel Schiötz (tenor) with Gerald Moore (piano)   HMV BLP 1064 (G.B.)
Lotte Lehmann (soprano) with Bruno Walter (piano)   Columbia 4 ML 4788
(U.S.A.) (Frauenliebe)

Frauenliebe und Leben (Op. 42)

Kathleen Ferrier (contralto) with John Newmark (piano)
Decca lw 5089 (G.B.)   London 5020 (U.S.A.)
Irmgard Seefried (soprano) with Werba (piano)
DGM 19112 (G.B.)   Decca 9971 (U.S.A.) (Mozart: songs)

Liederkreis (Op. 24) (Wolf: Lieder Recital)

Gerard Souzay (baritone) with Dalton Baldwin (piano)
Decca LXT 5216 (G.B.)

Liederkreis (Op. 39)

Dietrich Fischer-Dieskau (baritone) with Gerald Moore (piano)
HMV BLP 1068 (G.B.)   Victor LM 6036 (U.S.A.) (Side 4 of Schubert:
Winterreise)

Zwölf Gedichte (Op. 35) (Schumann: Miscellaneous leider)

Dietrich Fischer-Dieskau (baritone) with Günther Weissenborn (piano)
Deutsche-Grammophon DGM 18380 (G.B.)   Decca 9935 (U.S.A.)

DRAMATIC MUSIC
Manfred

Royal Philharmonic Orchestra, B.B.C. Chorus, conducted by Sir Thomas
Beecham   Columbia 2ML-245 (two discs) (U.S.A.) Fontana CFL 1026-7
(G.B.)

ICONOGRAPHY

Berlin State Library: pp. 151, 178
Paris Conservatoire Library: pp. 9, 143, 165, 187
Bulloz: p. 103
Giraudon: p. 49
Harlingue: pp. 85, 150, 174
Heinz Winkelmann, Zwickau: pp. 12, 53, 164 (Archives); 11, 22, 23. 25, 28,
41, 50, 68, 92, 95, 96, 120, 139, 146, 162, 175, 179 (Schumann Museum)
Roger Viollet: pp. 49, 101, 107, 113, 145
Stadtgeschichtliches Museum, Leipzig: pp. 46, 47, 59, 121
Staatliche Fotothek Museum, Dresden: pp. 6, 51, 63, 75, 140, 170
University Library, Tübingen: pp. 81, 82, 123
End-papers by Moritz von Schwind.

1455